S0-AGD-209

The First Valle Crucis

Seventh-day Adventist Church and Church School

And Other Mountain Stories

By
Ruby Clark Demyen

Ruby Clark Demyen
Demyen
2005

TEACH Services, Inc.
Brushton, New York

PRINTED IN THE UNITED STATES OF AMERICA
World rights reserved. This book or any portion
thereof may not be copied or reproduced in any form
or manner whatever, except as provided by law, without the written permission of the publisher, except by
a reviewer who may quote brief passages in a review.

2003 04 05 06 07 08 09 10 11 12 · 5 4 3 2 1

The author assumes full responsibility for the accuracy
of all facts and quotations as cited in this book.

Copyright © 2003 TEACH Services, Inc.
ISBN 1-57258-239-1
Library of Congress Catalog Card No. 2002108687

Cover Photo:
Ruby Clark Demyen's folk art painting of the first
Clark's Creek Church and schoolroom. It hangs in the
present Valle Crucis SDA Church.

Published by

TEACH Services, Inc.
www.tsibooks.com

Valle Crucis, cradled between the Watauga River and the Blue Ridge Mountains was named by an Episcopal Bishop, Levi Silliman Ives, who came to the valley in 1842 to start a mission. He saw the three creeks that intersected to form a shape of a cross and called the area Valle Crucis, Latin for valley of the cross.

Acknowledgements

I just could not abide—to use a mountain expression – the thought of memories of our first little church, church school and wonderful teachers being completely lost. Most of the independent, hard working, hospitable, home-loving mountain people who gave the North Carolina mountains their distinctive aura have been replaced by people from "somewhere else."

Descendants from the old pioneers are fast losing their mountain roots so I wanted to "set the story down."

I grew up in the Clark's Creek area of Valle Crucis and attended the Church School from 1919–1928 so I didn't come on the scene for 35 years after the beginning of the story. But, I remember my grandfather, Harrison Clark, and others telling about the beginning. I wish I had known then that some day I would regret that I had not asked more questions.

I'm grateful and want to say a big THANKS to all those who let me probe their memories, to people who joined me in my search of old records and family pictures, and who answered my letters with scores of answers to myriads of questions. In addition to those named in the book: Doris Bliss, J. Arthur Byrd, the late Clay Clark, the late Maude Baird Clark, Herman Davis, Erman Fox, Loy Fox, Silas Fox, Mildred Gwynn, the late Lester Hodges, Wanda Hodges, Pastor Ted Huskins, Betty Norwood, the late Lillian Shook, Louise Stout

Skidmore, Bertha Jestes Townsend, Raymond Woolsey, and Pauline Townsend Young.

I also want to recognize my daughter, Barbara Mullen, and son, Andrew Clark Demyen, for chauffeuring me up and down the mountain hollers to seek out information and photos. And last, this whole story could never have been finished without the long hours of my daughter-in-law, Jan Ohrmundt Demyen, who organized, edited and got my manuscript to print.

Author may be reached at:

Ruby C. Demyen
101 Granny's Bar Road
Hague, Va. 22469
804-472-2097
demyen@crosslink.net
(her son's e-mail address)

Chapter 1

The Valle Crucis Church and Church School

The Beginning

After the dawn in western North Carolina's Blue Ridge, the sun inched its way over the wreath of mountain tops and chased the heavy morning fog out of the narrow, rough "holler." On the hill overlooking the old fallen-in log cabin a lone cedar tree with dangling broken limbs marked the spot. The old rotting fence still guards the mossy, half-buried tombstones marking the graves of the early pioneers — but wait a minute. This sounds like the end of a story, not the beginning, so let's begin at the beginning.

The purpose of this story is to tell you about our Valle Crucis Church School and to preserve the memories of all the wonderful teachers and the roll call of the students who attended the school. But I couldn't do justice to the school story without first telling about the beginning of the church, which is a story all its own.

I want to tell you about the people who lived in that western North Carolina community — about the rough, narrow, crooked "hollers" and the well-beaten, wooded paths winding across the hills at the head of the hollers that shortened the distance for the people and students going to the church and school.

The events in my story began more than 100 years ago — about 1876. I have searched and searched for names and exact places of the first two people involved. **Lillian Presswood-Shook,** the grand-daughter of **William Jestes**, an early church pioneer, told me this part of the story but did not know the names and a fire in the New York Conference of Seventh-day Adventists office had destroyed early records.

A spark of hope found in an old The Youth's Instructor (church youth paper) faded out and left me having to say, "A lady from somewhere in New York State sold butter and eggs to pay for religious pamphlets and send them to an old-time mountain preacher who lived somewhere in the Blue Ridge Mountains of western North Carolina — Watauga County, to be exact. How she knew the preacher's name and address remains a mystery."

We do know the newly established Seventh-day Adventist denomination operated a publishing house and printed religious literature stating their beliefs and especially about the seventh day being the Biblical Sabbath day. Church members were urged to distribute this literature far and wide. A wild guess is colporteurs in the South selling Bibles and religious books from door-to-door may have sent names North requesting literature be sent to them.

The mountain preacher probably did not bother to read the literature but passed it on to some of his church members. Soon the Bible truths, especially the seventh-day Sabbath found in this literature, became the main topic of discussions carried on by clusters of men talking in the church yard after the Sunday church service, where men drew close to the fire in the country stores and as they talked together in their homes.

Eventually pamphlets fell into the hands of **Larkin Townsend, William Norwood, William Jestes, Monroe Baird, Harrison Clark** and **Samuel Kime** — all staunch members of their local churches.

Let me explain a little more about mountain people

Most people living in that area of the mountains were of Scotch-Irish descent whose ancestors

This photo shared by Ted Shook shows some of the first members of the southeast's first Adventist Church. L-r: Bill Norwood, Harrison Clark, Ellen Clark, William Jestes, Sarah Baird, Monroe Baird, and Haley Norwood in about 1924.

immigrated to America because they wanted to own land and have enough land for their children. Many first settled in the lowlands of North Carolina. After the Regulators War, brought on by unfair taxes and crooked deals from government land supervisors, they sold out and headed their oxen and wagons toward the mountains where they bought large tracts of low-priced mountain land. In spite of many hardships and with much hard work they cleared the land and tamed those mountains into farms — not the fertile farms of the Piedmont area — but they grubbed out a fairly decent living for their large families.

They planted apple orchards, hung grape arbors over rocks (let's not talk about the wine, apple jack, or moonshine some made), and obtained their milk, butter and cheese from cows they grazed on hillside pastures. Wool from their own sheep kept the spinning wheel swirling and knitting needles clicking. Big smoked hams cured in the smoke house. Chickens scratched around the kitchen door, ducks quacked around the barn yard and guinea fowl sneaked through the paling fence to catch bugs in the garden. A big gaggle of geese provided feathers for their feather beds.

Enough tobacco for their smoking and chewing needs dried in the barn loft. Big wooden barrels of molasses, sauerkraut and pickled beans filled the corners of the lean-to kitchens. Bins heaped with potatoes and ripening winter apples filled the bins in the dugout cellar.

And I must not forget the sweets — crocks of blackberry jam and apple butter waiting to go between hot breakfast biscuits on cold mornings. Also the glasses of apple, grape and gooseberry jelly hidden away to appear on the table when visitors came.

Not every family kept bees but my grandfather, **Harrison Clark**, was a bee man. Hardly a meal passed without a "spot" of honey to sweeten the end of the meal.

Aside from farming many mountain men were skilled craftsmen — carpenters, rock masons, blacksmiths, woodworkers and so forth. My grandfather made large wooden bowls turned on a lathe. My grandmother was a weaver.

Some men were millers who ground the corn and wheat on water-turned stone grinders. Others made chairs on water-turned lathes.

I know I have jumped the track a little from my church story but I wanted you to know these early pioneers were not nomads or ex-convicts but strong, able, hard-working men and women who with their families were contented with their life in the mountains.

Like other sections of our country, pockets of poverty existed — usually far back in rough, isolated hollers where men with poor judgment and little initiative would rather keep a pack of bony, half-fed hound dogs and hunt than to get ahead (as my mother said) by working hard. Families that pulled together and worked hard never had a lot of money but they always had plenty to eat and wear.

By hard work and thrift they had earned their independent, hard-headed way of living. Each man's politics and religion were strictly his own business — it was an unspoken rule that no one tampered with either one. Once a Democrat always a Democrat. Once a Republican, always a Republican. Only traitors crossed the line or sold their vote. Even when I grew up in the early 1900s, election day could turn into a gun-toting affair, bordering on the old Hatfield and McCoy days, as each party watched the ballot box for cheating.

New Bible truths reach the mountains

For these men, whose religion had been imparted to them by their parents, reading the literature sent by the lady from New York and studying their Bibles to change their day of worship was truly the working of the Holy Spirit on honest hearts.

After reading the literature and studying their Bibles they became agitated when their own church pastors could not give them a satisfactory answer about the Bible day of worship and they sent to New York for help.

This little story about the first men who kept their first seventh-day Sabbath was handed down to me by **Loy Fox**, grandson of **Harrison Clark** and **Columbus (Lum) Fox**.

On Sunday morning after keeping his first Sabbath **William Jestes** was feeling good about himself; he walked over three mountain ridges from his home at the foot of Grandfather Mountain to Matney community to tell **Monroe Baird** he had done so. He found Monroe working on his farm on Sunday because Monroe had kept his first seventh-day Sabbath the day before, too.

After a lot of enthusiastic talk and Sarah's good dinner under his belt he decided to go home by way of Banner Elk and stopped at **William Norwood's** home. William also had kept the Sabbath the day before and was working on his farm that Sunday. All three had kept their first Sabbath the same day without knowing about the others.

The men received a response to their request for help. Since I had never heard this piece of history from the memories of older church members, I will quote from the SDA commentary (Vol. 10, page 203): "**C.O. Taylor**, who had been one of the first SDA preachers in New York state, visited them as he and his wife traveled south in 1876 and conducted a series of evangelistic meetings at Shulls Mills, six miles from Valle Crucis. In 1879 a church was organized at Shulls Mills, Wautauga County, known as the Wautauga Church."

In 1880 the General Conference (church headquarters) sent **J.O. Corliss** to survey and foster the work in the south. He visited the members in the mountains and ordained **L.P. Hodges**, and licensed **Columbus Fox** and **Samuel Kime** as gospel ministers. Three years later he ordained Kime.

L.P. Hodges organized a little church on Dutch Creek, originally called the Bethel Church, May 15,1881 in the home of **Larkin Townsend** with 11 charter members. They were: **Monroe Baird, Samuel Kime, Larkin Townsend, William Norwood, William Jestes and Lum Fox**, and some of their family members. **Harrison Clark** believed in the seventh-day but did not join the Church until a little later. Also **Carson and Martha Aldridge Byrd** probably read the literature but decided not to give up their long-time membership in the Clark's Creek Baptist Church.

As new truths came to these church members their enthusiasm grew quickly. Families studied with their neighbors and soon a goodly company worshiped with them.

A year later in 1882 they decided to build a church. **Larkin Townsend** donated a narrow strip of creekside land across the creek from his home and Bob Hodges' general merchandise store on

Dutch Creek. Bob Hodges, Townsend's son-in-law, was the grandfather of the Hodges clan that belong to the present Banner Elk Church. (My mother told me about to going to Bob Hodges' general merchandise Store with her mother when she was a young girl to trade wild roots and herbs for merchandise such as cloth to make dresses.)

They build their first church

Church members walked long distances — some as far as 10 miles — to help build the church. The women brought big buckets of dinner to the men who started early in the morning and worked until dark. The men felled trees, hand-hewed the timber and mortised it together with wooden pegs. According to **Jake Norwood**, son of pioneer **William Norwood**, no nails were used in the construction of the church. They hand-planed, hand-grooved boards for the floor and ceiling. According to Jake, in spite of fifty years of winter snow and heavy rains, the shake-shingle roof never leaked.

They built the church only 64 X 14 feet, strong and sturdy like the faith and hopes of their new-found faith. This church is believed to have been the first SDA Church building in the southern United States.

Inside, two wooden lamp holders, one on each side of the hand-crafted pulpit, held kerosene lamps. Lamps in brackets on the walls lighted the narrow homemade benches.

Will Byrd told me the short little preacher's bench on the rostrum behind the pulpit is still in existence, stored in the attic of the old Egger's house nearby.

Ruby Clark Demyen's folk art painting of the first church on Dutch Creek. It hangs in the present Valle Crucis SDA Church.

No vestibule led into the little church. A few steps beyond the tottering footlog across the chattering creek, the only door opened one step up, directly into the building. On the far side of the narrow churchyard clusters of rhododendron, mountain laurel and spruce seedlings clung to the crevices of protruding rocks, and a rail fence separated the churchyard from the pasture and the rolling hills beyond the church. If you use your imagination a little you might envision ducks splashing around in the rocky waters as they searched for tender shoots of bulrush or wild peppermint.

Some folks believed in the seventh-day Sabbath but could not accept other SDA beliefs. For many people giving up eating pork, chewing tobacco and drinking coffee or an occasional nip from the corn liquor jug proved to be more difficult than changing their day of worship. To tell the truth, my mother told me some among the church members backslid into some of these old habits between revivals.

Often ministers and their wives came to the mountains and lived among the people — sometimes as much as two or three years — to help establish church members more firmly in their new-found faith and to keep the early church on course when the light of truth flickered and burned low. Also, living among the people proved to be a successful way to evangelize.

To put the organization of this newly formed church in its right setting in connection with other events in early SDA denominational history, I'd like to mention a few other dates and happenings.

1844-The big Millerite disappointment occurred when Christ did not appear for the Second Coming as many had expected.

1847- Adventists started keeping the seventh-day Sabbath.

1849- The first Present Truth, the church pamphlet about its beliefs was printed.

1851- The first Review and Herald (a weekly paper for church members) was published.

1863-The General Conference (a central governing body) was organized.

1881-The Dutch Creek Church was organized.

1901-The Southern Union Conference was organized and at that time North Carolina had only three ordained ministers, three licentiates, 10 churches, two companies and 300 church members.

1915-Ellen White, whose prophetic visions helped guide the early denominational organization, died, having lived 34 years after the Dutch Creek Church began.

Before the Southern Union Conference was organized, the General Conference considered the southern states a mission field. For years the only full-time workers were colporteurs going from door-to-door selling Bibles and religious books. A minister occasionally passed through visiting interested groups of people. Ellen White encouraged church members living up north to move south and help establish schools and small sanitariums.

Following is a quote from the SDA Commentary (Vol. 10 p.203): "**Samuel Kime** wrote in 1882 that there was no full-time minister in the state. In 1889, three years after North Carolina had been made a mission field, it had one minister for 80 members, mostly in the western part of the state, a state Tract Society and a Sabbath School Association." State conference headquarters were still called Tract Societies when I was growing up in the 1920s.

Soon after the Adventist Church on Dutch Creek was organized in 1881, evangelist meetings were held at Grandfather Mountain, Banner Elk, Cove Creek, Matney and possibly other places in Watauga County. Many people believed what the Adventists believed but prejudices and pressure from their long-established churches kept them from joining the Adventist Church.

Chapter 2

Meet The Men And Women

I'd like to tell you about some of the early church pioneers.

Larkin Townsend

Larkin Townsend was among the first men to discuss the church literature sent from New York, and he was the great-grandfather of the Hodges, Townsend and some Norwood members of the

Thanks to Isabelle Clark Rider and Wanda Hodges for sharing this photo of Larkin Townsend (April 15, 1832–June 21, 1922) and Mahala Townsend (July 15, 1836–July 26, 1925).

present-day Banner Elk Church. He and his wife, Mahala, lived on Dutch Creek where he and his daughter and son-in-law, **Sarah and Bob Hodges**, owned a country store. His little farm is known today as the Eggers place.

The first church was organized in his home and he donated the land for the first church building. A story handed down that several of his great-grand-children have reported hearing is that he could not read or write but taught himself to read so he could read the <u>Review and Herald</u>, the weekly Seventh-day Adventist Church paper.

The remodeled home of Larkin Townsend is in the background. Wanda Hodges and Ruby Clark Demyen in the foreground at the May 2001 centennial celebration of the Southern Union Conference.

L.P. Hodges

Very little information has been passed down from the memories of the early members of the first church on Dutch Creek about Elder Hodges. We do know he officially organized the church in the home of Larkin Townsend on May 15, 1881.

Wanda Hodges, great-granddaughter of Larkin Townsend, told me she had been told that the first group of men — **Larkin Townsend, William Norwood, William Jestes and Harrison Clark** — went to Sands, a community near Boone, N.C. to see a preacher soon after they made up their minds to worship on the seventh-day Sabbath. Since the Seventh Day Baptists had an active church in Boone for several years, I wonder if Hodges could have been a member of that church, and possibly a preacher there.

According to the SDA Commentary (vol. 10, p. 202) he was ordained as an SDA Minister November 20, 1880. The Lord used his abilities where and when He needed him.

Wanda says her family does not know if L.P. Hodges was an ancestor of the Hodges clan at the Banner Elk Church. She says he could have been but they are not sure. A search of tombstones in the old cemeteries in the Sands area and talking to families whose ancestors have always lived in Sands might be worth a try for more information.

Jefferson Rowe

I've heard my grandfather, **Harrison Clark**, speak of Jefferson Rowe as one of the early members of the first church on Dutch Creek. His son, **Washington Rowe**, and my father, **Roby Clark**, were good friends. I remember he often stopped to visit at our house long after he no longer attended the SDA Church.

My mother, **Maude Baird Clark**, told me Jefferson once lived on the little farm on Clark's Creek that the church later bought — in this story I often refer to it as the School Farm. For several years Washington Rowe or some of his descendants lived at the Dobbin Place on Hanging Rock Road in upper Banner Elk.

Jefferson was married to **Samuel Kime's sister, Mary Ann**, whose name is listed as one of the first members of the Banner Elk Church in 1912. She and another of **Kime's sister's, Marcia Jane Smith**, are buried near their parents in the Methodist Cemetery on the campus of Lee McRae College in Banner Elk.

Samuel Kime

Kime, who was about 23 and studying for the Methodist ministry, had already been licensed to preach. At first he refused the literature and shot back his share of arguments against the new beliefs being discussed. Later he asked for the pamphlets and promised to prove to the

Samuel Henderson Kime
(Nov. 18, 1851-Jan. 3, 1936)

people Sunday was the biblical day of worship. After reading them and carefully searching his Bible, he decided to join the other men who had decided to keep the seventh-day Bible Sabbath. He helped build that first church, was ordained as an

SDA minister in 1883 and pastored the fledgling church until about 1891 when he took his growing family and moved west.

As far as the sorrowful church members were concerned, the memory of their beloved pastor ends there. However, when Mrs. Marguerite Jasperson, principal of Fletcher School, interviewed Harrison Clark for her <u>The Youth's Instructor</u> story written in 1935, he told her Elder Kime was still living.

In the fall of 1998 new information about Elder Kime came to me. Now I need a whole chapter to tell you about him and his family and even so that will not do him justice.

Ellen Elizabeth King Kime (Dec. 25, 1855-Feb. 14, 1907).

Sharon Olene Manguson, great-great-granddaughter of Samuel Kime, lives in Alaska and plays the piano at the Eagle River, Alaska church. She came to Valle Crucis and Banner Elk digging for information about her great-great grandfather. She visited the two SDA churches, took pictures of my folk art paintings in the Valle Crucis Church and left me her address.

She sent me a whole packet of information including Samuel Kime's obituary. Her letter tells what sparked her interest in learning more about her great-great-grandfather: "When my mother passed away in 1996 I came across several items that she left, among them an old <u>The Youth's Instructor</u> article about Grandpa Kime and the old

Dutch Creek Church. I became fascinated by the story and other things I learned about my Kime family connections and planned the trip to North Carolina."

I learned from Sharon's letter that Samuel Kime was not one of the "passing through preachers" just visiting the Dutch Creek Church, but a native son of North Carolina born in Statesville. His parents moved to the Banner Elk area of Avery County after the Civil War. Quoting again from Sharon's letter: "While in Banner Elk I was able to find the graves of Elder Kime's parents, Wilson and Lydia Kime, and their daughters, Marcia Jane Smith and Mary Ann Rowe, wife of Jefferson Rowe, another early member of the Dutch Creek Church."

After Elder Kime left the mountains he lived in Viola, Idaho where he continued to evangelize and organize churches. He eventually ended up in California and Washington state where his children could continue their schooling. I learned from his obituary that most of his children became church workers. His obituary read in part:

"Samuel Henderson Kime was born in Statesville, N.C. November 18, 1851 and died Jan. 3, 1936 at the White Memorial hospital, Los Angeles, Calif. following a surgical operation. In his early years he learned to carry responsibilities and endure hardships."

"In his early youth he united with the Methodist Church, which communion granted him a preacher's license. At the age of 23 he came in contact with the teachings of Seventh-day Adventists, and gladly cast his lot with these people, thereafter giving his life to the promulgation of his newly found hope. Our brother was a pioneer, having attended the early sessions of the General Conference in the days of Elder James White, and before Elder J.N. Andrews went abroad as our first missionary."

"He labored in North Carolina, Tennessee, Oregon, Washington, Montana, and Idaho. He erected the first Seventh-day Adventist Church building south of the Mason-Dixon line. This building still stands at Banner Elk, N.C. His faith in the triumph of this message grew stronger with the passing of the years, and his star of hope never grew dim."

Monroe and Sarah Clark Baird about 1880

William Monroe Baird

To introduce **Monroe Baird** as one of the early church pioneers will take more space than a few lines.

After **Samuel Kime** moved west, **Monroe** became the local church Elder of the Seventh-day Adventist Church on Dutch Creek. For 40 years he pastored them—through their first love, they're backslidings and revivals, and their sad disappointment when they had to abandon their first church building in 1912.

After the church separated and two churches were built he pastored both the Valle Crucis and Banner Elk churches along with a small church on Cove Creek. (The last members, by the name of McBride, of that little church were still living as late as 1924.)

He preached at each church every third Sabbath. The Sabbath he was not at a particular church, the members met for Sabbath School, talked for a while in the churchyard, said their "Go home with me's" and went home.

Brother Baird, as he was affectionately called, was not an ordained minister but a good preacher and leader of the church. He worked on his small farm and shepherded the three churches. He did not baptize or perform marriages, but did preach funerals when the occasion demanded it.

He officiated at "quarterly meetings" (communion service), which were high Sabbaths at the church. Members too old or living too far from the church to come every week made a special effort to come on communion Sabbath. The church clerk read the names of each member from the church register and each member stood and testified as to their courage in the faith — that is, all except the shy ones. They just answered, "Present."

The men and women separated for the foot-washing before the wine and bread were passed. As a child I would get so tired sitting through the long service, but after the service the big "dinner on the grounds" was well worth waiting for.

For baptisms, which usually followed revival meetings in the fall after the work on the farms let up, the men and boys ponded up the creek. This sacred symbolic rite always seemed more real as the sins washed away, floated on down the creek.

As a young man, Monroe taught public school in Avery County, N.C. where he probably met and married **Sarah Clark Baird**. They lived on their small mountain farm, once a part of the large tract of land on the windy plateau above Valle Crucis (Matney community) that his parents, **William "Mountain Bill" and Sarah McNab Baird** bought before the Civil War.

Unless Sarah or Monroe's mother were going to church with him, he rode his big pied horse, Bob. If we, at Clark's Creek Church, saw old Bob tethered by the road below the church we knew Monroe would be at our church that day to preach. I remember seeing Monroe taking off his leather leggings as he warmed by the wood heater after his long ride in the freezing mountain weather.

Some of us Church School children liked to brag about how Monroe's mother and our great-grandmother **Sarah McNab Baird** had seen the stars fall in November of 1833. But since starting this story and comparing dates I have found she was born four years after the big prophetic event. She grew up when the new hope of the nearness of the Second Coming of Christ was fresh in the minds of the people. My mother told me Monroe's mother often went to church with him and thought of joining the Adventist Church. But her husband had donated the land for the Methodist Church and cemetery across the valley from their home and she had helped start that church — in fact she still was the "ram rod" of the church and couldn't "abide" the threat of being disfellowshiped.

Let me take a little break from the who, when and where of my story and tell you a little Civil War tale about Sarah McNab Baird from whom Monroe got most of his staunch genes.

Like many other mountain people at that time, **Mountain Bill and Sarah Baird** had little stake in the Civil War. When the rebel Home Guard came searching for Bill to force him to serve in the Confederate army or be hung, he hid out in an overhanging rock cave hidden in the steep Laurel thicket ravine below the intersection of what now is Highway 194 and Rominger Road. To keep from being tracked to his hiding place, Sarah walked on stilts when she took her husband his food. (I read about her walking on stilts on page 56 of Terry Harmon's book, The Harmon Family, which includes the Bairds.)

When my brothers and I were kids our **Alphonso Baird** cousins took us to find that cave. We scrambled and scratched our way down the steep ravine, through brush and laurel so thick in places we had to scramble over the top to find the cave. They pointed out the flat rock he had used for a table and bragged that he could hide so far back in the cave a match would not burn.

William "Mountain Bill" Carter and Sarah McNab Baird

In about 1980 I tried to find the cave again but the woods and rotting leaves must have reclaimed it.

Monroe staunchly professed his new religion. Sometimes he was accused of making a lot of noise working on Sunday to let people know he no longer worshiped on that day. But I remember being at the Methodist Sunday School with my cousins and hearing some rather heated, explosive arguments erupting from the men's Sunday school class he often taught.

This story would not be complete without telling you about Monroe's wife, Sarah. More than half the babies born in that part of the mountains owed their first breath to Aunt Sarah's first smack on their little behinds. Yes, she was a genuine mountain midwife. Not a Granny woman but a trained midwife. When the "time came" the neighbor women gathered in to have the tea kettle boiling while the new papa-to-be hie-tailed it to fetch Aunt "Sarrie."

About the year 1905, Aunt Sarah had help "borning" the babies. A new doctor, **H. B. Perry** setup an office in the back of Will Mast's store. He filled his saddle bags with the medicine and made house calls on horseback all over Watauga County.

He courted and married a pretty young school-teacher, **Doris Taylor**. (My mother, **Maude Baird Clark** was one of her students and remembers the doctor coming to the school house to see her.)

Doctor Perry built them a mansion of a house in Valle Crucis. Although later they moved to Boone, this house, with its long flight of steps is still there, near the intersection of River Road and Hwy 194.

I know I am straying again from my story but I'd also like to mention another beloved old country doctor — **J.B. Phillips**, one of the first doctors in Watauga County (1889–1923). Since he played an important role in the lives of the mountain people about the time of the first Dutch Creek Church, I feel he deserves to be mentioned.

I have heard my grandfather, Harrison Clark, mention "Old Doc Phipps," as the mountain people called him. He rode his horse and sometimes walked when necessary to care for his patients. This story goes that he often returned home with his boots frozen to the stirrups of his saddle and his wife would have to thaw his feet out to get him off his horse. (" The Harmon Family" Vol. 2, pg 74).

Monroe Baird's home at Matney, N.C. The house is still there but has been re-modeled and is no longer owned by the Baird family.

Monroe and Sarah Baird were noted for taking in needy people — those in trouble or who just needed a home for awhile. These people. many from outside of the mountains, seemed to find their way to the home of Monroe and Sarah.

Aunt Sarah could always be found helping to care for the sick in the community. That is where she found **Carl Oliver**, whose mother had died and he was about ready to breathe his last breath. She took him home, cared for him and she and Monroe gave him a Christian home, raising him as their own son. In his last days he became a faithful SDA Church member.

Here's another little story I heard.

In the 1980's my mother and I were visiting **Ona (Onnie) Byers**, another of Monroe and Sarah's foster children. She and Mama had been girlhood chums. They told me about the cobbled, rough brogans — shoes they wore when they were little girls. They were cobbled by the local shoemaker from rough, tanned cowhide. Each shoe fit either foot. When one shoe wore down on one side they just switched it to the other foot to get twice as much wear from one pair of shoes. The shoes often became hard and tight and rubbed blisters onto their feet. My mother developed corns and bunions that plagued her feet (from those homemade shoes) for the rest of her life.

As Mom and Ona talked, Ona asked if Mom remembered when Ona burned up her shoes. My ears perked up. I knew a good story was coming.

One spring day in May near corn planting time — the happy month mountain children always shed their shoes and long underwear — Onnie was limping along, wearing her misfitting old shoes, helping her "Papa," Monroe, clear the field for plowing. A big fire near the edge of the field burned old logs and trash.

As Onnie stood watching the fire burn, she decided she had had enough hurting from those old, hard, pinching, blistering, rubbing shoes. She sat down on the ground, jerked one shoe off and give it a sling into the fire. She curled her other foot, yanked off the other shoe and away it sailed into the hot coals. She stood there wriggling her freed toes and watched her shoes burn knowing full well they were the only shoes she owned.

For days afterward everyone in the family helped hunt for Onnie's shoes but only she knew those shoes would never be found.

Monroe and Sarah loved to go to camp meeting. Not only did they enjoy the meetings that slaked their thirst for newfound truths but, they loved the trip away from the mountains and meeting old friends year after year. Their earliest trips were made with ox team and covered wagons. How do I know about this? When I was about 12-years-old our church schoolteacher, Mrs. Burdick, took me to a camp meeting at Knoxville, Tenn. with her family.

She had charge of the junior tent meetings. For one meeting she asked Sarah Baird to tell about going to camp meeting by ox team and wagon. Sarah told about finding roads completely washed out — many times only answered prayers helped them complete the trip.

They probably went to camp meetings in Asheville, N.C. My reason for thinking this is that in a story written by **Marguerite Jasperson** (published in the March 15, 1935 The Youth's Instructor) she says **Robie Hodges**, then a member of the Banner Elk Church, told her when he was a little boy he had gone to camp meeting with his parents in a covered wagon pulled by oxen. They had gone to Asheville — a distance of over 100 miles and the journey took five days each way.

I have almost forgotten to tell you about the little one-burner iron kerosene stove Monroe and Sarah always took to camp meeting with them. They brought their own eggs, saved up and preserved in a crock of salt. They brought potatoes dug from their own patch and jars of apple jelly and blackberry jam, and made their own meals. (I wish I knew what happened to that little camp stove after Monroe and Sarah's deaths. It deserves a place of importance in the church history.)

While I am writing about camp meetings, let me jump the track again to tell you that **Arthur Byrd**, son of early church member **Hard Byrd**, told me the first camp meeting of the Carolina Conference was held on Dutch Creek. The people camped in their wagons in the meadow across the Creek from that first church building. Arthur was not sure of the date. A wild guess is that people came from "down in the country," around Hickory and Lenore, N.C.

D.T. Shireman, who helped build the Dutch Creek Church had started a self-supporting school and orphanage at Hildebrand near Hickory, N.C. that predates the organization of the Carolina Conference. **Monroe's daughter, Libbie**, helped take care of the children at the orphanage, which made it close to the hearts of the mountain people.

I remember being at camp meeting the summer after Monroe's death where so many of his old friends asked about him and said how much they missed him and his good Irish humor.

Two weeks before Monroe's death he preached his last sermon. For 40 years he had pastored the local churches.

I was 11 years old at the time and remember well the day of his funeral. The sun hid its face behind dark, misty clouds clinging to the mountain crests. Streaks of misty, gray fog ambled along Crabtree Creek, which ran through the valley meadow. Wagons, buggies and horses that brought people to the funeral churned the wet, thawing road into a river of slush and mud.

Throngs of people milled aimlessly around Monroe and Sarah's yard or talked quietly in groups saying in hushed tones — I can't believe this has happened. Many of them had walked miles since they had milked their cows early that morning. Members of both the Valle Crucis Church and the Banner Elk Church had lost their shepherd.

After his wife, Sarah, and two daughters, Monarky and Libbie, requested the casket remain closed at the church, the throngs of people stamped mud from their shoes and passed by the casket resting in the parlor of his home.

In those days, undertakers were few and sometimes far away. Immediately after a death, close neighbors came to the home to wash, dress and lay out the body. Large general merchandise stores like Mast's at Valle Crucis (now the Old Mast Store) usually carried caskets. On occasion, when Mr. Mast knew the family he would assist with the funeral.

Often the funerals were held at the deceased's home. But I remember hearing church bells toll, one dong for each year of the person's life for funerals of the more well-to-do families. For burials some distance from the church and cemetery, a wagon and team transported the casket.

For Monroe, men acting as pall bearers carried his casket the short distance to the nearby Methodist Church for the funeral.

Elder B.F. Kneeland, then-president of Cumberland Conference, expressed his admiration for Monroe and honored him by coming in person from Knoxville, Tenn. to preach the funeral. He came on the train (the Southern) to Johnson City, Tenn., then transferred to the narrow gauge train that came to Elk Park where someone with a horse and buggy met him. Because of the ankle-deep, churned up, thawing, muddy road, Elder Kneeland rode a horse to the Methodist Church for the funeral. He rode that high-stepping bay like a high-flying statesman. I can still remember seeing his gangling, long legs jammed into the stirrups, his usually long solemn face and long neck stretched above his rain slicker, wearing a black hat as the horse pranced along the grassy edge of the muddy road.

Monroe rests in the Baird family row at the churchyard cemetery of Liberty Methodist Church awaiting the Second Coming of Christ he preached about for so many years.

Clark family about 1896. L-r back row: Roby, Charles, Hardie, Nora. L-r middle row: Harrison, Wheeler, Ellen, Ada. L-r front row: Stella, Florence.

Meet Harrison and Ellen Clark

They lived with their seven children on Clark's Creek up near Nettle Knob. Their two-story log house covered with white, narrow weather boarding is no longer there. Only rocks from the

Pencil memory sketch of the log home of Harrison and Ellen White Clark. It was covered with grooved siding. The house was torn down and rebuilt on Hade Smith Drive in Matney community.

collapsed chimney mark the spot where it once stood. It was dismantled and the beautiful old hand hewn logs were taken to Hade Smith Drive in Matney and re-built into another log home.

The last time I passed the old place with fond memories dancing in my head, I took a rock from that old chimney to cement it into my sidewalk.

Harrison studied the literature sent from New York along with the other men and attended Church, but according to **Cora Fox Woolsey's** information he and Ellen didn't become baptized church members until the early 1900's. They had a hard time deciding if they could feed their big family without the big fat hogs they butchered every fall of

Ruby Clark Demyen's memory pencil sketch painting of the first Clark's Creek Church and school room

the year; there were possibly other forbidden habits that were hard to give up too.

I remember as a child I wondered why Grandpa Harrison always had his cup and saucer of steaming hot water with his breakfast — it replaced his

Clark family about 1917. L-r back row: Wheeler, Hardie, Roby, Charles. L-r middle row: Ada Clark Stout, Nora Clark Fox, Stella Clark Lowrence, Florence Clark Byrd, Etta Clark Stout. L-r front: Harrison and Ellen.

cup of steaming hot coffee after he became a baptized church member.

Harrison was the patriarch deacon in the Valle Crucis-Clark's Creek Church. In my memory I can still see him walk to the front of the church, hang his hat on a nail above the little bench at the front side of the church, then piously sit down.

Harrison always furnished the wine for the church communion service. He made his wine from grapes he grew along the top of the high paling fence around the garden. Ellen made the communion bread. (If I am allowed another memory here) she once slipped some of us curious grandchildren a taste of the bread left over from the service — it made us feel like we had sort of beat the ritual.

Harrison and Ellen had enough love in their hearts to make each one of us 32 grandchildren feel as if we were the most precious person in the world to them. Before I was a old enough to remember, my mother said I cried every Sabbath after church to go home with grandma. (I only remember the first time I didn't cry — but that is another story.) Going to Grandpa and Grandmas was always like going to a little heaven on earth.

Introducing Columbus (Lum) Fox and his wife, Martha Brewer

Lum and his big family lived only a short distance down Dutch Creek from the first church building. He was licensed to preach by **J.O. Corliss** in the year 1880. **Raymond Woolsey**, great grandson of Lum, has in his possession the cloth chart of the prophetic animals mentioned in the Bible, (Daniel and Revelation) that Lum used while going about the country preaching. After Raymond's grandfather, **Burt Fox**, died, his grandmother, **Nora Clark Fox**, thought Raymond should have it.

Columbus has faithful grandchildren in the SDA Church today that do him honor.

William and Haley Norwood

If you were able to shake hands with William Norwood you would miss a thumb on one hand. His grandson, **Stewart Norwood**, said he lost his thumb while cleaning his gun.

When I visited Stewart in 1998 he told me, as we thumbed the Norwood family photo album, William was a Union soldier during the Civil War and his neighbor, **Millard Arnette**, was a Confederate soldier. The two Army camps were near each other and the two men got together evenings, sat and talked about home for while before each one went back to his camp.

Stewart told me that William once lived in Dollars Holler near the Mast Store in Valle Crucis. I never knew he ever lived any place but Norwood Holler.

I treasured my visit with Stewart — his enthusiasm and help as he told me about his grandfather had encouraged me to finish this story.

To get to the church on Dutch Creek, William and his family walked from Norwood Holler above Banner Elk, across the rocky Hanging Rock Gap Road, then down upper Dutch Creek Road to the church.

The name Hanging Rock provides another little Civil War story I had heard but was not sure it was not another handed-down tale until my school-teacher cousin, Mildred Shook Smith, told me more about it. She said a Civil War battle was fought near Banner Elk and Pigeon Roost Road. A Union Army general was captured and hanged on the steep rock at the top of the mountain peak. Also, a soldier killed in that battle was the first person buried in the Banner Elk Presbyterian Church cemetery.

Today it's hard to believe that once the mail was carried across the Hanging Rock Gap Road on horseback. I remember seeing the deep grooved scars in a slanting rock left there by the wheel of the first car the mail carrier attempted to drive across Hanging Rock Gap sometime in the 1920's.

After the organization of the Banner Elk Church, William, in spite of the long distance from his home in Norwood Holler to the church in downtown Banner Elk, faithfully attended church until he became too old and blind to make the trip.

William never ceased to pray for his wavering grandchildren.

William (Uncle Billy) and Haley Norwood

William (Billy) and Mary McClurd Jestes

While making one more effort to find a picture of Jestes I received a letter from his grandson, **Ned Jestes**, and learned how William came to be living in the rough narrow Valley at the foot of Grandfather Mountain.

The letter said, "My old uncles told me the tale of how William Jestes met his wife Mary. After the Civil War, while returning home to Buncombe County (after being discharged from the Union Army) and scouting to avoid the so-called Confederate Home Guard, he looked down from the top of Peak Mountain and spotted the smoke from a log home almost surrounded by huge trees on the north side of Grandfather Mountain.

He told his companion, "I think I will go down and meet the man — he must be kin to the devil to live in such a place."

Three months later he married McClurd's oldest daughter, Mary Milishia who was only 15 years old. He worked closely with his father-in-law, Billie McClurd. They soon built a log house near the present Jestes cemetery. Living was very hard for honest, Christian people who had little except their

Ned Jestes, grandson of church pioneer William Jestes, talking with the author about his grandfather.

hands to carve fields from the virgin forest. My grandmother, Mary, told me the first summer they were married they lived on ramps, woods greens, cornbread and fish she caught from the river. The country was very isolated and primitive. The land, except for cleared fields up the mountainsides, remained as the resource for sustainable farming.

"Billy farmed on the McClurd land and reared nine children to adulthood. He converted to the Seventh-day Adventist Church and helped establish the church on Dutch Creek. He always rushed the boys to finish the fall work so he could travel through western North Carolina to promote his beliefs and sell books written by those in the Adventist Church. He was gone for months on this missionary work."

Billy walked over two mountain ridges to help build and attend the church on Dutch Creek. After the church divided and two new churches were built, he faithfully attended the Clark's Creek-Valle Crucis Church until he became too feeble to walk the long distance. Even then, by using his cane he managed to get there for Quarterly Meetings (Communion Service) and when visiting ministers came to preach.

I remember he would leave his home early in the afternoon, come by our house for supper and go on to the church with us.

A few years after his death, one of his young grandchildren said to a group of us children, "Grandma Jestes (Mary) prays every night for the little church on Clark's Creek."

What a tribute to the church and to the memory of her loyal, faithful, pioneer husband.

Early Visiting Ministers

During the years following **C.O. Taylor's** visit in 1879 and **J.O. Corliss'** visit in 1880 with the first group of seventh-day Sabbath-keeping men, from time to time other ministers came to the mountains to help the fledgling church — some stayed as long as two or three years or even longer and lived right among the people, which seemed at that time the most effective way to evangelize.

According to information gathered from **Cora Fox Woolsey, Maude Clark, J. Arthur Byrd and Harrison Clark** these are the names of some of the those ministers:

Elder W. H. Armstrong and his wife, Gertrude, lived about 1912 among the mountain church people for three years or more while he evangelized. Gertrude taught a two-family church school in the home of **Hard and Roetta Byrd**. She also taught a church school in the new Banner Elk Church (see church schools on page 48). Elder and

Mrs. Armstrong's names appear on the first Banner Elk Church register in 1912.

D.T. Shireman (pronounced Sherman), once a brick mason, carpenter and engineer, turned a self-made, self-supporting church worker. His work eventually brought him to North Carolina during the last part of the 1880s. He helped build the first church building on Dutch Creek and stayed around to help stabilize the fledgling church members as they learned the new truths of their new found faith. Elder Shireman willingly gave himself to organizing churches and establishing self-supporting schools throughout the southern states. One often mentioned in our church was the orphanage he established at Hildebrand near Hickory, N.C. Monroe Baird's daughter worked there helping take care of the children.

How an angel protected Elder Shireman from falling about 100 feet over the Dutch Creek Falls when he slipped on a slick rock above the falls, made a deep impression on the mountain people. This oft repeated story has strengthened the faith of many young people, especially those in the church who liked to walk to the Falls on Sabbath afternoons.

Elder Nash, according to my mother's memory, lived right in the home of my grandparents, **Harrison and Ellen Clark** before he finally convinced them they could do without coffee and could feed their family of seven children without the hogs they butchered every fall of the year.

Elder W. L. Adkins was another minister who often came to the mountains to hold revivals. He preached the last sermon in the old Dutch Creek

Church building in 1912 when the congregation separated and built two new churches. His straightforward, plain-spoken sermons drew crowds to his evangelistic meetings. He became the mountain people's beloved preacher. When my grandmother, Ellen Clark, died the family called him to preach her funeral and later to preach my grandfather's funeral.

After Elder Adkins retired he bought the church-owned school farm and pastored the waning Valle Crucis Church until his death. He is buried in the Fox cemetery among the people he loved.

Marvis Adkins Kilgore, his daughter, shared this information:

"My Father was Walter L. Adkins. Born in 1880 in Cambridge, Md., he came from a Methodist heritage. The men in his family were watermen and built Bug-eye Boats and Skipjacks that sailed the Chesapeake Bay.

"When he was about 18-years-old he heard an evangelist and became a Seventh-day Adventist. He left home (actually he was disowned and turned out), went to Washington Missionary College in Takoma Park, Md. and became a Minister and evangelist. They held tent meetings in those days.

"He married and had a son, Clayton. His wife died after five years with typhoid fever. In the early years he was in the Maryland area but gradually came further south. He married my mother, Neva, in Goldsboro, N.C. in, I think, 1915. Louise was born in Savannah, Ga., I was born in Roanoke, Va., and our brother, Walter Leroy, was born in W.Va. It was all this area that made him fall in love with the mountains and the people. It was a love that never left him.

"In the early '30s my father had a terrible accident—he was hit by a bus. I was very small at the time. He was in a coma for days and never really regained his health after that "So he moved back to a place he loved, to live out his days. It was Clark's Creek and Valle Crucis where he pastored the Clark's Creek and Banner Elk Churches. The Church was up on the hill from the Clarks but I see it is now in Daddy's bottom land. I used to play down there near the creek and pick flowers. When I was up there last fall (2000) I was so glad to see the barn still standing.

"The house looks beautiful. The corn crib is gone and that's OK. He was in the barn when he had his heart attack in 1947. He is buried up on the hill at the Fox Cemetery. It is so beautiful and where he would want to be. His headstone says, "Asleep in Jesus." I am sure when he opens his eyes at Jesus Coming he will so happy he has been there all these years.

"One thing I do remember is I think he was very instrumental in getting electricity up into Clark's Creek. I remember that was a very exciting time for folks there. Everyone was so happy to have radios at last."

Chapter 3

New Churches Form

The second churches

After worshipping in the Dutch Creek Church for 30 years, by the year 1912 the congregation had grown and there was a decision to build two new churches in place of it – one in Banner Elk and a new one on Clark's Creek.

The **Norwoods, Townsends, Hodges** and other members living in the Banner Elk area decided to build their own church because of the long distance they had to travel to get to the Dutch Creek Church.

Then the **Clarks, Foxes, Byrds, Jestes and other Townsends** on the Clark's Creek side of the ridge took the opportunity to build a new church on Clark's Creek near Valle Crucis.

Banner Elk Church

The church members living in Banner Elk built their church on a beautiful, level, beech tree-shaded lot covered with fluffy, wild grass on the road between Banner Elk and Balm (now Route No. 194). The plain building with clapboard siding and a shake-shingle roof did not have a belfry or a steeple, (I checked this information with Lester Hodges), but an inverted vestibule lead through double doors that opened into the church sanctuary.

Pencil memory sketch of the first Banner Elk Church about 1912. Later it was turned sideways to accommodate the new highway and made into a private residence. Now it's a Bed and Breakfast in the old Banner Elk business section.

The red velvet-decorated pump organ beside the pulpit with a round lamp holder awaited the footwork of the schoolteacher or the wife of a visiting minister.

A little path beside the church lead to a small, slanted, two-holed outhouse that hung over the bank of the little creek behind the church.

In 1929 the first Banner Elk church building was sold and a building more centrally located between the members in Norwood Hollow and the members in Banner Elk was built on the site of the present day Banner Elk Church.

Today's Banner Elk Church and school

The new owners of the old church turned it to fit the narrow lot left after the highway department took the back end of the land when they straightened out old 19E (now Highway 194). They remodeled it into a nice two-story residence and today it is a bed and breakfast establishment in Banner Elk's prosperous downtown business section.

Today the old church building is an up-to-date Bed and Breakfast establishment in downtown Banner Elk.

Valle Crucis Church

The church members on the Clark's Creek side of the ridge left their beloved little church on Dutch Creek to build a church on Clark's Creek just over the steep ridge from Dutch Creek and about a mile above Valle Crucis. These sons and daughters of the earliest church pioneers, put their inborn mountain skills to work and built a church they could be proud of, on a knoll overlooking the creek and the adjoining valley meadow.

Locust logs were hewn into solid, long-lasting foundation sills. They put on a split-shingle roof. Hand-grooved clapboard siding painted white covered the outside of the church. But the crowning glory was the large, square belfry attached to the right front corner of the church building. Fancy woodwork adorned the bell tower that housed the big bell and a tall straight steeple pointed to the sky.

On Sabbath mornings the sound of that bell could be heard up and down the valley and echoed in the hollers long after the tall, white steeple could no longer be seen. The church became, not only a landmark in the community, but also a witness to the faith and hope in the soon-to-come return of Christ.

Inside the church the high ceilings and walls were finished with hard, black pine, grooved and varnished to a shine. Iron bracketed lamp holders attached to the walls between the windows held flat-bottomed kerosene lamps with ruffled globes. The pulpit with a preacher's bench and podium were all stained dark oak, a strong contrast to the hard, maple floors and pine ceilings. This pulpit and podium were considered the most sacred part of the church. Only Elders and ministers used it.

The Sabbath Superintendent and Secretary sat in cane-bottomed chairs beside a small square table below the pulpit. They would never think of using the podium. It has always been a little hard for me to except Sabbath School conducted from the pulpit.

The pump organ had red velvet lining covering the sound holes. The congregation was always glad when the schoolteacher or a visiting minister's wife was there to play the organ. **Burt Fox**, son of **Lum Fox**, knew how to keep time to the hymns and led the singing.

He stirred up some hard feelings among the congregation by occasionally stopping the singing to impart self-important criticisms about keeping the right time to the music. I remember once when **Elder Monroe Baird** had had enough of the criticism and told him to go crawl under the back seat and listen while the congregation would show they could sing without him.

The deacon's bench occupied the space along the wall on the other side of the podium. After the schoolroom was built on, a big sliding door made of matching grooved pine, separated the two rooms and could be opened to extend the church when needed.

I've saved telling you about the church benches until the last. These benches were the pride and joy of the men who built the church. Even though I probably eased my cutting teeth as a toddler on the high backs of these benches, swung my tired legs and feet back and forth under them before my legs were long enough to touch the floor, and later cast shy glances at the slightly slouched teenage boy I was "struck on," I never heard this story of how the benches were made until **Arthur Byrd** told me about them in 1996. He was about eight or nine years old when the church was built.

The timber for making these benches was cut from big, virgin hemlock trees growing on land owned by **Hard Byrd** in the area below Dutch Creek Falls known as Falls Flat. I have seen stumps of these big trees. For many years, rows of corn planted near them had to go around them before they finally rotted.

Since Falls Flat was near the Valle Crucis. Mission School saw mill, a wild guess is that the big hemlock logs were taken there and sawed into rough, wide boards. **Hard Byrd and Burt Fox** designed and built the benches. It must have taken a lot of help and hard work to hand plane these boards smooth.

They were constructed with only one long, wide board for the seat and one for the back. Mortised into the extra thick arm rests and held tightly with wooden pegs, they were so sturdily built they did not need brackets attached to the floor to hold them solidly in place. They proved to be sturdy yet comfortable. According to **Arthur Byrd,** these church benches were so well-liked, other churches asked **Hard Byrd** to help build their pews.

The young people always liked to sit in the very back pew of the church where a little side door opened into the belfry and out to the side of the church. They could sneak in late unobserved and could slip out during the closing song when that fitted their purpose.

The church on the steep bank was torn down in about 1960, but these sturdy-built benches are still being used in the present church building built at the lower corner of the valley meadow. If you visit you may wonder about the back of the very front bench — just half as tall as the other pews. One of the teachers had her husband saw that back in half so she could see what was going on in the rest of the room. I remember feeling sad because anyone would dare to alter one of those most sacred benches.

Good-bye to Dutch Creek Church

Even though they had two new churches, older church members could not pass by the little, abandoned church building on Dutch Creek without a tinge of sadness as they told us children, "That's the old Adventist Church."

For 28 years it stood abandoned by the creek. The gray, hand-hewn clapboard siding slowly succumbed to age and weather. The clapboard shingles curled their edges. No footsteps rattled on the shaky narrow footlog to cross the Creek. Tall, untrampled grass and weeds encouraged the pasture to reclaim the old churchyard. The door stood open and sheep sheltered themselves from the weather inside the old church.

But the disastrous mountain flood of 1940 changed everything. It completely washed away the old building. Not one splinter of wood or stone was left to mark the site where it had stood by the creek. Only memories were left. When my generation passes even the memories will be gone.

Chapter 4

More On The Church School

Getting back to the story of the church school

Just recently, while picking the memories of **J. Arthur Byrd** and **Cora Fox Woolsey**, I learned about a small school taught in the home of **Hard and Roetta Byrd**. They lived at the foot of Nettle Knob in the last house on Clark's Creek Extended Road. **Gertrude Armstrong**, Pastor Armstrong's wife, taught the **Byrd boys — Rennie, Fred, Donald and Arthur — and the Fox girls — Cora, Verdie and Estelle (Essie)**. The **Bert and Nora Clark Fox** family lived in an added-on-to log house at the lower side of the big rock near the Clark's Creek Bridge.

The date of this little school is a calculated guess — probably about 1910 and the church was still located on Dutch Creek.

After completing their new church building the Valle Crucis Church members added an ell for a church school room that was ready for classes in 1915. They wanted a school where a Bible class could be taught along with the three Rs.

Also because of the long distances the children had to walk in the severe winters the "free school" (public school located near the old Baptist Church — actually across the road from what is now **Johnny Byrd's** fish pond) taught school only four months a year. Another reason for the short school year was the families of the older boys could not spare them from the work on the mountain farms until after the work was "done up" in the fall of the year, and they had to leave school early in the spring to help with planting.

Here I would like to let **Cora Fox Woolsey** tell her story about the beginning of the Church School in a letter she wrote to me in 1989.

"It was about this time (when the school room was almost finished) I decided to try to go to Camp Meeting. I was told if I went I would have to take my sister, Verdie, with me. I was working for a family in Banner Elk — housekeeping and caring for the children — for \$2.50/week.

"When the time came to go to camp meeting I had earned enough money for our train fare and had gotten our needed clothes. I went home the evening before we were to go, to get ready to go to Camp Meeting. (She probably walked from Banner Elk over to Hanging Rock gap, down Dutch Creek, then over the next ridge to Clark's Creek, a distance of about 6 to 8 miles.) Papa announced he was going to Camp Meeting with us if he could get the money. I had two dollars I had not spent. He took that and found enough more and was ready to go with us. We soon learned why Papa came. He was looking for a teacher to start school in a month.

"He persuaded a young lady by the name of **Myrtle Maxwell** to come to the mountains to teach that first Church School.

"The school room was not finished but school started in the church using church benches for desks. In a few weeks all was finished and we had a real school in the nicest building in that part of North Carolina."

First Church School in the Carolina Conference

This was the first real Church operated Church School in the Carolina Conference supported by the Church, not just some parents.

Now let me tell you about the schoolroom. A long panel sliding door made of finished pine that matched the interior of the church separated the schoolroom from the front side of the church. Slightly opening this long door allowed the school-room to be used for children's Sabbath School. When slid all the way open the schoolroom became an extension for the church when needed. By sliding this door part way open the organ in the front corner of the church could be used by the school.

Three big windows on each side of the school-room matched the windows in the church. Wide, smooth, boards painted black were across the front of the room and served as the blackboard. A few years later regular blackboards were installed across the front and along one side of the room.

Dog-eared, creased maps hanging above the blackboard were unrolled for use as needed, and a round, whirling globe of the world were the only teacher aids in the room.

A small long-legged square table with a pencil sharpener attached to one corner and with a small drawer housing the teacher' s pencils served as the teacher's desk. A small hand bell sat on top. (That table, coated with scaling black varnish, is now used in the vestibule of the present church.)

The school desks were made from left over lumber — mostly oak, pine, poplar or chestnut. The desk seats were attached to the front of the desk behind them. The height of the seat determined which grades sat in them — lower ones for wiggly, leg-swinging first and second graders and higher seats for lanky, slouching, long-legged older boys. A long church bench across the back of the room served as the first seat for the back row of desks.

When I was going to school an ink-stained, knife-notched desk made of poplar was my favorite.

Two students sat at each desk, which made a nice cozy situation when you were six years old and the person sitting with you was the same age and your best friend. But beware of too much whispering or giggling or you might end up with a new seat-mate.

A long, high backed church bench in front of the teacher's table served as the recitation bench. The poor teacher had to stand up to see over it and what went on in the rest of the room. One teacher, Mrs. Burdick, solved that problem. She had the back of that bench sawed in half. If you should you happen to visit the present church, you will notice that little bench occupies an honored position as the first bench at the front of the church.

A small, partly closed-in porch connected the outside entrance to the schoolroom and led to the belfry where firewood was stored. Coats and caps hung on long nails, and overshoes were left in this porch room. A water bucket and dipper were also kept there.

I bet you can never guess what else was on the porch — at least during my school years. The older boys carried meal sacks of shelled corn slung across their shoulders as they walked to school. At the morning recess they took these "turns" of corn to Mr.

Jackson Townsend's water mill located just below the Rock Jumping falls. At noon time they picked up their sacks of corn meal, left them in the porch-cloak room until the end of the school day and then shouldered them home. "Mr. Jackson" usually helped the boys by bringing their sacks of corn meal up over the rocks from the mill to his house.

I have almost forgotten to mention the big, long, iron wood heater in the middle of the room. Oh, how many children got scolded at home when their father found they needed new soles for their shoes because they put them too close to the heater while warming their feet after their long walk to school. **Betty Young Norwood** remembers how good frozen apples tasted thawed out on that old iron heater.

The first year **Myrtle Maxwell** taught the first school in 1915 she boarded with church families.

The old school farmhouse in the background is now painted and well kept up. The foreground is the present Valle Crucis Church

By the beginning of her second year of teaching, the church members, as a way to financially secure continuing the Church School and to provide a home for the teachers, bought the small farm across the creek from the church. It included a valley meadow, woods, a garden plot, fruit trees and a hillside pasture. The meadow gave students the largest and nicest playground in the county.

To help pay the teacher's salary each family made pledges according to the amount they were able to pay. This often backfired when big families could not afford to keep their pledges. The poor chairman of the School Board was left holding the bag.

One of the highlights of the summer for the men and boys was "putting up" the hay on the school farm. They brought their horse-pulled mowing machines and hay rakes, pitch forks, mowing scythes, and homemade sleds pulled by horses to haul the hay to the stacks.

The second year Miss Maxwell set up housekeeping in the farmhouse and boarded several children who lived too far away to go back and forth to school every day. Some of these children were **Thuthel McGinnis, Iola and Mabel Jestes**. Their parents brought food for the children — probably potatoes, apples, canned fruit, pickled beans and sauerkraut from their dug out cellars, and molasses and dried fruit. The **Fox girls (Cora, Verdie and Essie)** along with Miss Maxwell's sister who lived with her, helped take care of the children. Her father also visited often.

Near the end of the second school year the faculty of Southern Junior College (now Southern Adventist University) at Collegedale, Tn., were hunting for a good teacher to head their Normal Department. Ms. Maxwell accepted the position and for several years trained some of the finest schoolteachers in the Seventh-day Adventist denomination. But she never lost her love for the people of the Valle Crucis-Clark's Creek Church and her students in that first school.

I think you'll enjoy **Cora Fox Woolsey's** version of what happened: "About the time Southern Junior College was moving from Graysville, Tn. to Collegedale, Tn., **Prof. Leo Thiel** was looking for good teachers. He came to the Valle Crucis Church School to see what we had and invited Miss Maxwell to come to Collegedale. Four or five pupils in the eighth grade at Valle Crucis would not be able to finish.

"She began promoting Collegedale. **Wheeler and Etta Clark, Cora Fox and Rennie Byrd** decided to go to Collegedale with Miss Maxwell. **Etta Clark's** family would not hear of her leaving home and she changed her mind.

"Wheeler's folks never gave up on him. They told him the war was on and he would have to come home anyway. They never realized he was such a bad cripple with his paralyzed arm that the Army would never have him. Finally Wheeler won and he, Cora and Rennie set out for Collegedale.

"But letters kept following **Wheeler** from his family and he finally came back home.

Rennie got homesick and also came home. When school started at Collegedale that fall **Cora** was the only one from the Valle Crucis Church who finished the eighth grade."

Note: **Cora** finished school at Southern Junior College and later she and her husband, **Arthur Woolsey**, went to China as missionaries.

Forgive me for butting into my story again to try to tell you why mountain people hated to see their children leave the mountains. Most were descendants of honest, dignified, peaceful Scotch-Irish immigrants. But they were tired of the ravages of religious and political conflicts and had a burning desire to own land and live where their religion and politics were their own business. Years of hard work had gone into taming the harsh, rugged Blue Ridge wilderness into self-sufficient farms. Their roots went deep and they were fearful of seeing their children leave their mountain homes because they usually never came back.

Once people left the mountains and came back to visit their families they were considered, "just coming in," and even though they always left a part of their hearts there, they could never really belong to the mountains again.

My great-grandmother, **Sarah McNab Baird**, put that feeling into words when she said of me after I left home at 15 to go to the Academy, "She will forget who she is." She begged my mother to bring me home but Mom was determined I should have the chance she never had of going to school.

I finished at the Academy in 1934 at the age of 17, then went on to nurses training at Mountain Sanitarium Hospital in Fletcher. After graduating in 1937 I worked in New England Sanitarium and Hospital near Boston, Mass., moving to Washington D.C. at the start of WWII to be nearer my brother who lived there.

The railroad brought our visiting ministers and school teachers to the Foscoe Depot in this valley and took the church families out of the mountains to church camp meetings... or on to a life outside the mountains.

I met and married my husband, Andrew Demyen, and we raised our two children there. It wasn't until we were both retired that we moved back to my beloved mountains in 1975.

Back to Miss Maxwell – I'm so pleased to be able to enclose a copy of the REMEMBRANCE from Miss Maxwell and the first school. A short time ago a member of the **Charlie Clark** family found this copy in their attic. **Clay Clark** had gone to school to Miss Maxwell about 80 years ago.

Another lucky break came my way soon after I started writing this story. While researching my Clark family history I wrote to my cousin, **Louise Stout Skidmore**, for information. She sent me an old picture. To her it was just an old picture of people she never knew. But for me it was a prized find for the book — a picture of Miss Maxwell and the students of that first Church School. **Etta Clark Stout**, her mother, had been one of those first pupils.

For information about the next two teachers who followed Miss Maxwell, I have scoured the memories of **Cora Fox Woolsey, Clay Clark, Arthur Byrd, Loy Fox and Maude Clark**. But none of these folks remembered the teachers' first names. For information about some of the last schoolteachers I have used the memories of **Will Byrd, Silas Fox and Betty Young Norwood** to calculate dates and ages from what I already knew. So some of this information is an educated guess.

1915–1917 **Myrtle Maxwell**

1917–1918, **Mr. Arkabour** (? spelling) and his wife came from Michigan according to Clay Clark.

1918–1919, **Mr. and Mrs. Collins** were both teachers from Michigan and probably knew the Arkabours.

1919–1920, **Mr. Climer**

1920–1922, **Olive Medford**

1922–1924, **Roberta Ingraham**

1924–1926, **Mary Burdick**

1926–1927, **Olive Medford**

1928–1929, **Charles Anderson**

1929–1930, **Hazel Fox**

1930–1931, **Fred Palmer**

1931–1932, **Dorothy Pierce**

1932–1933, **Mrs. Wellman**

1933–1940, **Clarence Wellman**

1940–1941, **Mr. Niverson**

1942–1945, **Marie Holloway**

1945–1946, **Mrs. H.H. Strickland**

◀ Left– Valle Crucis Church School children in 1915. Teacher Myrtle Maxwell, center, surrounded by her pupils. L-r back row: Wheeler Clark, Cora Fox (married name Woolsey), Rennie Byrd, Miss Maxwell's sister, Fred Byrd, Earnest Fox. L-r middle row: Mabel Jestes, Clay Clark, ?, Dare Lowrence,?,?, Don Townsend. First row, seventh from left Howard Lowrence.

Chapter 5

The Teachers

Mr. Climer

Mr. Climer, his wife (their first names have been lost to memory, four children (Earl, Dorothy, Ruth and a baby) and a grandmother lived in the farmhouse across the meadow from the church and school.

His six-year-old daughter, Ruth and I were seat-mates and I learned more about having fun with someone just my age than I learned about first grade reading.

Mr. Climer didn't finish out the school year, the reason for which I never knew. I do remember his patience with a roomful of school children of all ages and grades seemed a bit short.

Olive Medford Clark

As a young girl living in Michigan, Olive Medford prayed for the Lord to use her in some way in the work of the Church. (She told me this part of her story in about 1970 while we reminisced about when she taught me in the first grade. She was a friend of the Collins family and probably came with them from Michigan.)

The school with students, from dreamy-eyed, shuffling first-graders to smart-alec seventh and eighth graders, all in one-room at the Valle Crucis Church School, became her first challenge. Her school supplies consisted of a set of roll-down maps, a box of chalk and a pencil sharpener fastened to the table that served as her desk.

New books were usually purchased for the oldest child in the family, then year-by-year handed down to the next sibling in line. In large families, by the time the books reached the last child, they were pretty well beat up. Ms. Medford spent hours after each school day preparing color books and crafts and pictures for all the raffia-covered picture frames we made. She did all this along with planning lessons and outings for the older students.

Her morning devotional stories and prayers were reflected in her devoted Christian concern for all her pupils.

I'll never forget when she taught us how to pray. One Wednesday morning, following one of our special young-peoples' meetings, she left the older students in the schoolroom to wrap tracts for mailing as a missionary project. She told us first and second graders to follow her.

She led us out the door, across the little porch, through the belfry and to a seat between two high benches at the back of the church. As we scrounged and elbowed our way to find a place to sit on one of the long benches she said she wanted to teach us to pray. She told us we could talk to Jesus just like we talked to our fathers and mothers and that He would hear us. We could ask Him to bless our mamas and papas and missionaries in the foreign field and we could ask for His help when we needed it. She had each one of us say a short prayer. Those of us too shy to try, repeated the words after her.

Prayer became very real to me. In spite of a bit of teasing I unabashedly prayed my way out of many difficulties. So many times in later life I have longed for that childish faith in prayer that I learned from Miss Medford.

Forgive me for one more little personal story. After a long washing rain — a "freshette" — had caused the creek to overflow its banks, Miss Medford, knowing we might have a problem getting home, let my cousin and me out of school early. When we came to the creek crossing where splashes of fast-flowing water almost overflowed the foot log, we were afraid to try to cross. We decided to kneel down and pray about it.

When we arose from our knees, I crossed the narrow, dangerous foot log without a tremble. But my cousin, still afraid, found her way up through the field so she did not have to cross the creek.

Olive Medford's school years were not all peaches and cream. That one room had its share of rough necks, show offs and show-downers from those rowdy mountain boys. The worst escapade I can think of is the water bucket story. (I will not give names because these boys — now old men — are still living.)

The older boys were assigned, two by two, to carry the drinking water from a spring near the teacher' s house. For some unknown reason, when their turn came to carry the water, two of the boys were peeved because they had to do it.

On the way back across the meadow they stopped and urinated in the water bucket.

A School Board member living near the school who thought the school could not operate with out her and kept an eye on things at the schoolhouse, saw them and hurried to tell the teacher. But she didn't make it in time before several students and the teacher had a drink of that water.

We expected Miss Medford to wale the living daylights out of those two boys — and she could have — but she chose to stretch out the punishment.

She kept them in their seats every morning during recess and whacked the ruler over the palms of their hands every day for a week. It must have worked for their tear-stained faces were hidden in their arms on their desks when we came in from recess.

One of the big mountain boys, **Roy Byrd**, who usually caused his share of trouble in the school was not always so bad. How do I know?

Once when my seven-year-old seat-mate and I were trying to get across the flooded creek to go to the outhouse at the edge of the meadow, this big rascal of a boy saw our dilemma, grabbed us under each arm, took a long-legged jump and set us down on the other side of the creek. I have never forgotten his chivalrous kindness.

During her first year of teaching Miss Medford lived in the home of **Hardie and Zettie Clark**, just below Clark's Creek Bridge (on the lower side of the big rock you can't miss). She slept in a cold upstairs room in their old added-on-to log house. When the wind blew hard, snow sifted in through the cracks.

The second school year she lived with the **Hardie and Roetta Byrd** family and walked, come rain, snow or cold mountain windy weather, the long distance from the head of Clark's Creek to the school. That is, until **Wheeler Clark** decided it was too much for her and asked her to marry him. She became Aunt Olive to most of us schoolchildren and cousin Olive to others.

She tried to fit right in with her mountain kin and made Wheeler a good wife. Yet, a hint of being "from somewhere else" made her a little different. She never adulterated her Michigan accent with mountain lingo. She never swapped her good healthy homemade yeast bread for mountain hot biscuits and corn bread.

They lived with Wheeler' s parents where their first son, Grant, was born. In the fall of 1924 they moved to the Norwood settlement in Banner Elk where Olive started a new Church School.

Dear old Uncle **Billie Norwood**, grandfather of the Norwood clan, though old and blind welcomed them with tears streaming down his cheeks. He said he had been praying for the Lord to send someone to start a Church School and help revive the slowly dying Banner Elk Church. The people built a rough, one-room schoolhouse that had to be enlarged after the first month of school.

The Cumberland SDA Conference headquarters sent a minister to hold revival meetings that resulted in a large number of baptisms and re-baptisms. In fact one of our faithful old souls was re-baptized so many times one evangelist teased the Church Elder saying, "The only way some of these back-sliding members would get to heaven was if they were taken there immediately after being baptized." (Not so different from today, is it?)

But the Church never really stabilized to become the strong Church it is today until a new church was built on the present site, halfway between Norwood Holler and downtown Banner Elk.

After two years of teaching the new Church School at Banner Elk, Wheeler and Olive moved back to Clark's Creek with his parents. That summer death claimed their first small son and a second son was born.

That fall, when asked to teach the Valle Crucis Church School again, Olive said, no. She did not want to take another baby to school with her. But when the middle of September 1926 rolled around with no teacher for the school, she was persuaded to teach that year. She took her baby to school with her for the first two months until her mother came from Michigan to live with them.

At the end of that school year Wheeler and Olive moved into their new home on their own little farm. Another son, Vern, was added to the family and she became a full-time homemaker. (For any of you history chasers, their house is located across the road from the old, old Baptist Church near where **Johnny and Mae Byrd** now live.)

Since a mountain custom was for the youngest son to take care of his parents in their old age, Wheeler and Olive lived near his parents until their death in 1929. Then they finally decided to sell their little home on Wheeler's beloved Clark's Creek and move to Sand Mountain, Ala. where Olive started teaching Church School again. She continued her education, going to summer school at Southern Missionary College (now Southern Adventist University), and taught school throughout the Southern Union Conference until she retired.

After she retired they followed Wheeler's yearnings and moved back to his beloved mountains. They lived in the little village of Foscoe, across the mountain from Wheeler's old home place. Olive taught a Sunday School Class at the local Christian

Church at Foscoe, and wrote short articles for the Church paper, the *Review and Herald*.

But she missed teaching. She confided to me that she missed someone to talk with about something besides gardens, cows and chickens.

Eventually age and cold mountain winters forced Wheeler and Olive to move near their son and in Portland, Tenn. The last time I visited them there, she sneaked me a preview of hymns and music she was writing. She poured her heart out to me saying, "Oh, if only I had just 10 more years to finish all the things I want to do." Sadly she had only three more months.

Herman Jestes, one of her very first pupils at the Valle Crucis Church School expressed the thoughts we all wished we could put into words when he said, "If anyone ever deserves a place in heaven when Jesus comes again, that person is **Olive Medford Clark**."

Roberta Ingraham

I was nine when the little narrow gauge ET&WNC (Eastern Tennessee and Western North Carolina) train, later affectionately called Tweetsie, that ran from Johnson City, Tenn. to Boone, N.C. deposited Mrs. Ingraham and her three sons at the Foscoe Depot with all their bags and baggage. **Baily** was a tall, lanky 15-year-old red head, **Edward** was 13 and handsome, and **Preston** was blond and good-hearted. **Burt Fox** met them with his wagon and horses and brought them over the steep mountain road to the Church School farm where soon they were settled into the old farmhouse.

Later, two girls also lived with the Ingraham's — **Leslie Watson** and **Helen Allen** who later married **Donald Byrd**.

Mrs. Ingraham, a fairly large, well-dressed, professional-looking woman proved to be a very capable teacher. She taught the first nine-month school year — a few students in the 9th and 10th grades in the one room. How did she manage this? She taught grades one through four in the mornings while the older students studied. Then she sent the young children home at noon and taught the classes for the older students during the afternoon. She took a lot of interest in taking the students, especially the older ones, on hikes and field trips.

Her one woe was dealing with "Toughy," a boy who thought his duty was to maintain his reputation for out-doing all his teachers. His reputation went ahead of him to all the new teachers. He was a middle child in a big family of 12 children and probably used his actions to gain attention. He stubbed up and refused to mind his teachers.

During a tussle when Mrs. Ingraham was giving him a needed switching, he fell against the corner of a desk and cut his head. On the way over to her house to staunch the blood and patch him up she met his hysterical mama coming lickity-split, wiping her soap sudsy hands on her dangling apron and moaning, "Oh, what have you done to my poor boy?" You would have thought he was always a saint.

One of his younger brothers had run to tell his mother. Mrs. Ingraham had held her stand with Toughy — but she had more patching up to do than just the cut on his head.

A young teacher, **Blake Head**, taught the public school that year and organized some real rousing baseball games between the older boys in the

Church School and public school. Everyone wanted to play baseball. Some of the younger boys spent their evenings unraveling their mother's old cotton stockings and winding the thread into baseballs hoping they would be allowed to play. The boys shaved their own baseball bats using a stick of Ash wood.

The free school bell and the Church School bell rang every morning about the same time. Both schools were part of the community and often joined together for community doings — box suppers, pie suppers, and Thanksgiving and Christmas programs.

I remember a Thanksgiving play put on by Mr. Head. He included parents in the acting and they loved it. You would be surprised at the natural acting talent found among some of those mountain people. For weeks after the program folks teasingly mocked and chuckled about the actors in the scene of John Alden's courtship in the old Plymouth Colony.

In spite of the lack of modern conveniences, Mrs. Ingraham's boys loved their two years living in the mountains from 1922 to 1924. They became good buddies with **Forest McGinnis** who rode a horse followed by two big collies from Cove Creek to the school, a distance of 8 or 10 miles. The Ingraham boys often rode double on the horse to go home from school with him.

Besides being a good teacher, Mrs. Ingraham was an asset to the whole area. She became friends with the teachers at the Valle Crucis Mission School. The Watauga County School Board appreciated her interest and encouragement in their efforts to consolidate the County schools and asked her to speak at their meetings.

Mary Burdick

Mrs. Burdick and her husband, **Jessie** had two children — **Gordon**, who was in the third grade and **Esther**, who was in the first grade. **Allie Jenkins** and **Hazel Teague** boarded with the Burdick's.

The Burdick's made the trip from California to Valle Crucis in a little over one month in their old Star car, camping along the way. She came to teach the Church School and he worked as a carpenter with the **Clark brothers (Charlie, Roby and Hardie)**.

The Burdick's soon made themselves right at home in the old farmhouse where they used kerosene lamps, carried their own water from a nearby spring and cut their own wood for their tin heater and cook stove. Their home soon became a hospitality center.

Almost every Sabbath, a family was invited for dinner and to sample Mrs. Burdick's whole wheat bread. They celebrated birthdays or any other occasion with a party. They visited people in their homes, ate dinner with them and soon sorted out who was related to whom among the 30 children attending the school.

As a teacher Mrs. Burdick was strict but fair. She taught and disciplined with love and prayers. Her students responded by doing their best. Her thoughtfulness went beyond traditional school rules. For instance, she gave us each a candy stick to suck on while she read to us.

She made time to read to us especially after noon recess while we rested from hard playing. I remember one book vividly — John Williams, ship builder and missionary to the South Sea Islands. She made this story so real some tears were shed when Williams was finally clubbed to death by cannibals.

Mrs. Burdick was astounded at how little we students knew about our own North Carolina history — or, as a matter of fact how little we knew about the world in general outside of our own chimney smoke. We knew about county elections (sometimes a gun-toting event) and read news reported in the <u>Watauga Democrat</u>. She made it a point to read us books about North Carolina history during story time.

This memorable teacher encouraged promptness with monthly prizes — sometimes just a handful of English walnuts.

We sang a lot during morning worship and each student was encouraged to testify, telling what he was thankful for. Students took part in the Morning Prayer, each saying a sentence. She usually called the roll after the hymn singing so students coming late because of morning chores or having to walk along distance, would not be counted tardy.

During the first school year Toughy the trouble-maker attempted to maintain his reputation of out doing all his teachers. When Mrs. Burdick asked him to stand and read his theme for English class he refused to obey. She and everyone in the room knew a showdown was in the making.

She took his theme, read it, assured him he had nothing to be ashamed of, and urged him to stand and read it. When urging failed, Mrs. Burdick cracked the sliding door between the Church and the schoolroom, left us all alone and went into the Church. Toughy and every other student in the room knew she had gone in there to pray. You could have heard a pin drop in that room while she was out.

When she returned and again asked Toughy to read his theme he resisted a little, one more time, to save face, then stood up and read his theme. Mrs. Burdick had won. Everybody relaxed and went back to their studies.

Like a good general, Mrs. Burdick assigned the work of caring for the schoolroom to the students. The older boys took "month about" (that is, each took one month) coming early to school and building the fire in the big iron heater, then tending the fire throughout the day.

They usually brought a few sticks of kindling from home. This did not mean they had to carry all the wood. Each student was expected to carry a stick of wood up the steep path to the belfry each time he came from the playground.

Cutting the wood for the school was a project for the men and boys in the church. On a set Sunday they met in the latest new ground being cleared and cut wood. The men who had horses and wagons or sleds hauled the wood to the school.

Here in my story is a good place to tell you about birch bark brooms. Mrs. Burdick kept insisting the boys make some brooms to scrub the wooden floor — it was probably her way of including a craft in their studies while at the same time filling a need.

In times past these shaved wooden brooms were used to scrub the hard wooden floors in the ancient log cabins. The floors would be sprinkled with white sand, scrubbed with the brooms, then the sand was rinsed off with clear water.

Now, I can hear you thinking, "Where in the mountains did they get white sand?" Well, veins of pure white, fine sand could be found in certain spots — usually near brown shale rocks. Our farm above Clark's Creek had a "white sand hole" where people came to scrape out buckets full to clean their floors.

To make a birch broom, one end of a smooth, straight, broom-length small White Birch limb was sliced into shavings about one foot long. These shavings were then bent back over the end of the limb and tied to make the broom bristles. The rest of the limb was whittled into a broom handle. Usually only White Birch was used for the same reason the Indians used it for canoes — the wood is pliable, yet strong.

When the boys finally brought their scrub brooms to school they stacked them against the door so they would fall in every direction when the door was opened. All of the students took their seats and waited. As she neared the school Mrs. Burdick wondered why there were no students outside waiting for her.

When she opened the door, scrub brooms tumbled all around her. Everyone clapped. She said she was glad no one was outside to see her take a spill coming up the slick hill (slicker than usual that day because the boys had been riding their home-made sleds down the path.)

The scrub broom stunt pleased her so well she gave each of us a peppermint stick to suck on while she read us an extra story.

Another of Mrs. Burdick's unusual surprises was having school in the woods. One balmy, early spring day after Bible classes were over, she tucked a few books under her arm, picked up her hand bell and told the students to pick up their readers and spellers, grab their dinner buckets on the way out and follow her.

We crossed the creek and meadow and followed her up into the woods. She sat down on an old fallen log and announced we were having school in the woods. She said we could do anything we've pleased as long as we gathered for class when she rang her bell.

Boys headed for trees they could climb. Little girls started gathering log moss for a playhouse on a big flat fern-dotted rock. Older girls joined hands and started hunting for Hepaticas — little purple-tinged white flowers — the first to push their little fuzzy buds up through the rotted leaves.

Others searched over by a little spring for the first short-stemmed, yellow Johnny-jump-ups. Groups of happy students relayed to others when the peal of the ringing bell meant class was being called.

Then, after our dinners were eaten in favorite spots in the woods, Mrs. Burdick let us go home early while everyone was feeling good and happy about having school in the woods.

The two years the Burdick's lived on Clark's Creek were also good years for the Church because young people stayed in the Church. Families feuded less about the school. Members of other churches in the community loved the Burdick's and had a softer heart toward the Church. The Watauga County

School Superintendent took an interest in our school and paid us a visit.

Mr. Burdick did his part too when our beloved local pastor, **Monroe Baird,** passed away. Monroe had been a strong leader for both the Banner Elk Church and the Valle Crucis Church for over 40 years. His passing left both congregations like sheep without a shepherd. Preaching didn't come naturally to Mr. Burdick but he did his best to fill the void.

Charles Anderson

Charles and Ruby Anderson were newly weds from Hensdale, Ill. Ruby and **Evelyn Howe** were sisters.

Charles and Ruby came to Valle Crucis looking for **Clifford and Evelyn Howe** so I need to explain how the Howes came to be at Valle Crucis.

Mr. Howe told me this story about a year before he died in the late 1980s. He had studied to be a minister in college, then had gone to Hensdale Sanitarium to become a registered nurse. Next he and his wife traveled to Knoxville, Tenn. looking for a mission field. The Cumberland Conference president told them he knew just the place for them. He couldn't pay them a salary but he would give them a train ticket up to Valle Crucis where they could teach the next year at our Church School.

They arrived with the intention that Mrs. Howe would teach but she was expecting her first baby and one member of the School Board decided she should not teach. So they moved to Banner Elk to help the new school just starting there.

The Howes loved the people in Norwood Holler and they in turn trusted the Howes. For several years after the school was discontinued the Howes remained in the area and helped make the Banner Elk Church the strong Church it is today.

Now back to the Andersons. They had walked across the rough mountain road from the Foscoe Depot. I still chuckle about the beautiful floor lamp Mr. Anderson carried with him — it was probably a cherished wedding present. Little did he know the great distance to the nearest electrical outlet.

They stopped at our house, the first one they had seen since leaving the depot, to ask where they could find the Howes. My mother told them where the Howes had moved and put them up in our company bed for the night. The next morning they hitched a ride on the truck to Banner Elk when my father drove to work.

What a surprise when they came back with my father that evening. Mr. Howe had talked Mr. Anderson into teaching the Valle Crucis Church School. The School Board agreed and the Anderson's moved into the old farmhouse, bought a few chickens and a cow, and school started on time.

Since Mr. Anderson had taken nurse's training, **Miss Ruth Atwell**, the SDA Conference Education Supervisor, suggested he teach anatomy and physiology to the two boys in the ninth grade. He also was a cook and taught the older girls cooking. I still have my free Rumford cookbook he ordered for us; and for years it was the only one I had.

He took us to the farmhouse kitchen to practice our cooking. I remember making a green tomato pie with a crust so tough a knife couldn't cut it. The other girls teased me unmercifully and mortified me by threatening to take a piece to the eighth grade boy I was stuck on.

Like all eighth graders we liked to play games involving partners — especially when the right partner chose you. Our favorite was cat paddle, a ballgame with two batters, two catchers and two fielders.

We also had some lively games playing sheriff and outlaws (We girls always liked to be chased by the boys, eh?!). Once that game almost got out of hand when the outlaws hid in an old caved-in cellar in the bank of the road and the sheriff smoked them out.

Those outlaws came out sputtering and fighting mad. The teacher almost had to lock everyone up before tempers finally cooled.

Being the only girl with three boys in the eighth grade spoiled me. I lacked competition both socially and academically. When I went on to the academy I had a hard time holding my own, competing with a large group of students.

Hazel Fox

Hazel Fox, a daughter of **Bert Fox**, head of the Fox clan in the Clark's Creek community, had attended Southern Junior College and later graduated from Watauga County High School. At that time she was working on her teacher's certificate.

Some parents did not send their children to Church School that year because they felt her father had put her up to teach as a way to even the score with some of the Church Board Members with whom he feuded.

That situation, along with being closely related to almost everyone in the Church did not make for a healthy situation for her. Nevertheless, she taught a good school and later became one of the best teachers in the County school system.

I wish I had more information and dates for the teachers that followed Hazel Fox. After I finished the eighth grade I left the community to go to the academy and did not know the next teachers. My guesses are calculated from what I know about the ages of the children near my age. I apologize for any miscalculations.

Fred Palmer

Mr. Palmer lived in the old farmhouse with his wife and children. He taught school and pastored the Church.

Dorothy Pierce

Dorothy and Felia Pierce were on leave from Pisgah Academy. Felia traveled and sold religious books. Fannie Norwood from Banner Elk lived with them, went to school and helped care for their four children 6-years-old and under.

Mrs. Wellman

Mrs. Wellman was a dignified, well-dressed, older pastor's wife who came back to teaching to fill the need.

Clarence Wellman

Clarence and his brother Wallace were college students living with their retired parents during the time. Between Mrs. Wellman and her sons they taught school until about 1940.

Mr. Niverson

I was unable to find out any information about this teacher.

Marie Holloway

She was a young lady just becoming a teacher.

Mrs. H.H. Strickland

Mrs. Strickland and her husband had purchased a little mountain farm far up a holler and had rough roads to travel to get to Church and the School. She taught the last school year with only six pupils.

Eventually the 31-year-old, scratched, ink-stained, knife-whittled desks were donated to the Morganton, N.C. Church School.

Chapter 6

Conclusion

Within the last several years changes have come to the little mountain communities. Consolidated schools and busing have forced the County to better maintain the back roads. Today buses scramble up the deepest hollers and over ridges to pick up the schoolchildren at their door. Most of the children expect to finish high school. Many will learn a good trade at junior colleges. Better transportation and scholarships have put graduating from Appalachian University in Boone within reach of anyone who is willing to make the effort.

But the biggest reason for change was the devastating mountain flood in 1940 that demolished all the bridges and washed out all the narrow, crooked, old wagon roads — and yes, Tweetsie, the little narrow railroad that still ran one train per day from Elk Park to Boone. The state was forced to build better roads, then straighten out the curves, widen and pave good roads leading in an out of the mountains.

The good roads provided an outlet to good jobs, "down in the country," for young families trying to scratch out a living on the crowded little mountain farms. As **Ephraim Fox**, grandson of early Church member **Columbus Fox**, expressed the situation — He wasn't goat enough to make a living on those steep hillsides.

The same good roads opened the freshness and beauty of the area to tourists who swarmed to the

High Country for its perpetual cool air. Bulldozers wrapped ribbons of roads around the ridges and peaks, and summer homes and cabins sprang up like mushrooms.

Eventually property prices went sky high and so did taxes. Old-time people once so contented on their little farms could hardly afford the taxes. So when people from "somewhere else" offered them exorbitant prices for their little farms they jumped at the chance to get out from under their hardships— they sold out and moved somewhere else.

One by one, as death claimed the old Church members and one by one families sold out and moved from the area, fewer and fewer pews in the old church were filled. Inexperienced teachers or wives of older ministers filled the gaps in the teachers position of the waning Church School. The School farm often became a place for older and sometimes problem ministers to be put out to pasture, so to speak. None of them brought new life to the old Church or School.

In the mean time Watauga County replaced its one-room schools with consolidated schools that had longer school-years, certified teachers, school buses, and better facilities such as libraries, lunch rooms, gymnasiums and so forth. The Church School, as one student later described it, became a "one-horse school." After the 1945–1946 school year with only six pupils, the school closed.

With a heavy heart I have to tell you the present church in the lower corner of the valley meadow has replaced the old church. The steep path from the road up to the church became too difficult for older members and yes, hearses.

Today the tall pointed steeple no longer points to the sky. But the clear sounds of the same old bell can be heard on Sabbath mornings atop the present Church. And I'm glad to say the proudly built old hemlock benches fill the new Church, though a new coat of varnish couldn't hide all the knicks and scratches we children left on them.

When you visit the church you may wonder about the bench in the front row with its back just half as high as the other benches. Then remember the story I told you about Mrs. Burdick who had her husband cut the back in half so she could see what was going on in the back of the room.

The pulpit in the present church is not the one from the old church. Mrs. Marguerite Jasperson took the old one to Fletcher Academy where a fire destroyed it.

I can hardly believe the cracking, dried out, deteriorating short bench in the little side room in the present church is the once sacred elder's bench from the old church and the black, varnished, cracking, square table in the entrance of the church once served as the teacher's desk in the old school room.

This may not interest everyone but some of the beautiful ceiling boards from the old church are stored in the attic of the present church — care to climb up and take a look?

A cemetery surrounded by a high chain link fence helps keep the site of the old church as hallowed ground.

Not one Clark, and only two Foxes and two Byrds still appear on the old mail route. But the crowning insult is the name of our dear little Clark's Creek

Road that followed the creek has been changed to Justice Road. I guess the post office has its reasons but I sure don't like them.

All these changes have also affected the little Adventist Church down by the creek. Like most other little country churches that once dotted the hollows and hilly ridges in the high mountains, only a handful of hopeful members huddle into one corner of the Valle Crucis SDA Church on Sabbath mornings. I should say with one exception — the yearly homecomings when the little churches fill and run over with people yearning for the good old days, coming from near and far, laughing, hugging, reminiscing and feasting on the "dinner on the grounds."

A new church has been a organized in Boone. I hope they will accept the challenge and take up the flickering torch to continue the 112 years of Seventh-day Adventist presence in Watauga County. Who knows, some day troublesome times may force Christians to find a refuge in the mountains again.

Neither the handful of faithful members who tenaciously hang on at the old church nor all the people scattered far and wide who cut their teeth gnawing on those high-backed church pews and who learned the three "Rs" sitting at those old wooden desks, can bear the thought of the church not always being there.

Appendix I

Banner Elk Church record of November 23, 1912

1-Larkin Townsend
2-Liddie Norwood
3-Charles Hodges
4-Robie Hodges
5-John M. Calloway
6-Charlotte Calloway
7-Minnie Norwood
8-Sarah Hodges
9-Sallie Andrews
10-Jake Norwood
11-Wesley Norwood
12-Missouri Hodges
13-Hattie Hodges

14-Barbara Townsend
15-Elder W. H. Armstrong
16-Gertrude E. Armstrong
17-Mary Rowe
18-Daisy Andrews
19-Mettie Hodges
20-Lulu Norwood
21-Walter Norwood
22-Fred Norwood
23-Robert Calloway

Appendix II

Descendants of the pioneer Church members

This incomplete list of who married whom in that early Church and community is for descendants with a wee drop of Adventist blood in their veins who are searching for their mountain roots.

Monroe and Sarah Clark Baird's children:
Monarkey married Pless McGinnis
Libbie married Ebb Cannon

Harrison and Ellen Clark's children:
Nora married Berton Fox (son of Columbus Fox)
Charlie married Cira Foster
Ada married Will Stout of Tennessee
Roby married Maude Baird (niece of Monroe Baird)
Stella married Wilson Lowrence (a Baptist Church member)
Wheeler married Olive Medford
Florence married Dexter Byrd (grandson of Carson Byrd)
Etta married Wyley Stout of Tennessee

Columbus (Lum) and Martha Brewer Fox's children:
Roetta married Hard Byrd (son of Carson Byrd)
Burton married Nora Clark (daughter of Harrison Clark)
Phillip married Eliza Harrel, Charlsie Allron, Janette Ducker, and Margie Flanery
Jenny married John Owens
Addie was an invalid and never married
Dulcie married Vance Byers

William (Billy) and Mary McClurd Jestes' children:
Eliza married Bart Porch
Jane
Rebecca
Martha

Joseph married Minni Byrd (daughter of Carson Byrd)
Tempa
Cosaba
Jesse married Rose Byrd (daughter of Carson Byrd)
Robert married Julia ?

William and Haley Norwood's children:
Wesley married Lulu Townsend (granddaughter of Larkin Townsend)
Haley
Lydia married Jim Townsend (son of Larkin Townsend)
Jake married Lydia ?

Larkin and Mahala Townsend's children:
Lonnie married ?
Sarah married Bob Hodges (grandparents to the Hodges, members at Banner Elk Church today)

Samuel and Elizabeth King Kime's children:
Stewart
Kenneth
Walcott
Mettie
Minorks
Libbie Kay
Naomi
(Samuel had two stepsons and two stepdaughters from his second wife, Cora)

Other marriages in the community

Benjamin Byrd, son of Carson Byrd, married Rhoda Townsend, granddaughter of Larkin Townsend.
Fred Byrd, son of Hard and Roetta Fox Byrd, married Grace Calloway, daughter of John and Lottie Calloway, members of Banner Elk Church.

Appendix III

Gravesite locations

This information about where to find the graves of the church's pioneer men is for descendants who never had a chance to love our mountains, or for anyone else who would like to search for these old graves.

Monroe and Sarah Baird are buried in the Baird Row in the Matney Liberty Methodist Church graveyard. From the village of Valle Crucis take Highway 194 (once the Valley Mountain Turnpike). Go by the Mission School and up the steep, winding road that levels off at Matney community. The Church is slightly above the fork of Highway 194 and Rominger Road (may now be named Hill Road).

If you are coming from Banner Elk, take Highway 194 through Balm and over Bowers Gap. When the roads level off you are in Matney community and the Methodist Church is on the right near the fork in the road.

While in this area you might be interested in Monroe and Sarah's old home. It is the first house on the left going down Rominger Road near the firehouse. The place is no longer owned by any of Monroe's family. It has been remodeled some since Monroe and Sarah lived there.

Harrison and Ellen White Clark are buried in the Fox Cemetery on Clark's Creek Road going across the mountain to Foscoe. From the present SDA Church take the mountain road a short distance to the second curve. A path across the field leads to the fenced cemetery near the woods. Loy Fox still lives in a mobile home behind the old Bert Fox place and may help you to find the cemetery.

William and Haley Norwood, Larkin and Mahala Townsend and Columbus and Martha Brewer Fox are buried in the old Dutch Creek cemetery near the head of Dutch Creek. This cemetery will be hard to find because woods have almost re-claimed the land and no path leads to it from the road. It's located on a slanting wooded hillside to the right of Dutch Creek Road just before the turn off onto the once road and now trail leading across Hanging Rock Gap. A great-grandson of Larkin Townsend (whose name is also Townsend) lives a short distance down the road from there and would likely know the exact location.

William and Mary McClurd Jestes are buried in the Jestes cemetery in Grandfather Community located above Foscoe village on Highway 105, a short distance from the present Baptist Church. Their old house stood on the other side of Highway 105 but is no longer there. Ned Jestes, Billy's grandson, lives in the valley below the cemetery and I'm sure would assist you in finding the graves.

Samuel Kime is buried in Mount Hope cemetery near Los Angeles, Calif.

Jefferson Rowe, I think, is buried in the Methodist Cemetery on the Lee McRae College campus in Banner Elk. His wife, Mary Ann, and her sister, Marcia Jane Smith (sister of Samuel Kime) are buried there.

Appendix IV

Teachers and their students — Valle Crucis-Clark's Creek Church School 1915–1946

Teacher, Myrtle Maxwell 1915–1916:

First grade — Everett Fox, Mabel Jestes, Viola Clark, Lillian Coffey, Earl Townsend.

Second grade — Ray Coffey, Bertha Jestes, Roy Townsend, Lelia Davis, Beatrice Coffey, Howard Lowrence

Third grade — Roy Byrd, Iola Jestes, Dair Lowrence, Alma Byrd, Nellie Davis, Forest McGhinniss.

Fourth grade — Ira Fox, Hazel Fox, Clay Clark, Clarence White, Essie Fox, Ernest Fox, Grace Calloway, Donald Townsend.

Fifth grade — Arthur Byrd, Donald Byrd, Thuthell McGinnis, Fred Byrd, Edna Mae Trammell, Rennie Byrd.

Sixth grade — Virdie Fox

Eighth grade — Cora Fox, Wheeler Clark, Etta Clark, Rennie Byrd

Teacher, Mr. Arkabour 1917–1918

Clay Clark, Viola Clark, Fred Byrd, Donald Byrd, Arthur Byrd, Alma Byrd, Roy Byrd, Estelle Fox, Ernest Fox, Hazel Fox, Ira Fox, Everett Fox, Paul Fox, Cecil Clark, Donald Townsend, Roy Townsend, Earl Townsend, Grace Calloway, Dair

Valle Crucis S. D. A. School
Valle Crucis, North Carolina
1917

Φ

Myrtle Vivian Maxwell,
Teacher

School Officers

H. E. Clark   Chairman
J. B. Fox   Roby Clark   Sec. and Treas.

PUPILS.

FIRST GRADE

Everet Fox   Viola Clark
Mabel Jestes   Lillian Coffey
Earl Townsend

SECOND GRADE

Ray Coffey   Lelia Davis
Bertha Jestes   Beatrice Coffey
Roy Townsend   Howard Lowrance

THIRD GRADE

Roy Byrd   Alma Byrd
Iola Jestes   Nellie Davis
Dair Lowrance   Forrest McGhinnis

FOURTH GRADE

Ira Fox   Essie Fox
Hazel Fox   Ernest Fox
Clay Clark   Grace Calloway
Clarence White   Donald Townsend

FIFTH GRADE

Arthur Byrd   Fred Byrd
Donald Byrd   Edna Mae Trammell
Thutbill McGhinnis   Rennie Byrd

SIXTH GRADE

Virdie Fox

EIGHTH GRADE

Cora Fox
Wheeler Clark   Etta Clark

Valle Crucis SDA school roster of 1917

Lowrence, Howard Lowrence, Ed Lowrence, the Davis children and the Coffey children.

Teachers, Mr. and Mrs. Collins 1918–1919

Clay Clark, Viola Clark, Claude Clark, Cecil Clark, Donald Byrd, Arthur Byrd, Alma Byrd, Roy Byrd, Estelle Fox, Ernest Fox, Donald Townsend, Hazel Fox, Ira Fox, Everett Fox, Paul Fox, Roy Townsend, Earl Townsend, Grace Calloway, Doris Calloway, Georgia Calloway.

Teacher, Mr. Climer 1919–1920

Clay Clark, Viola Clark, Claude Clark, Cecil Clark, Ruby Clark, Donald Byrd, Arthur Byrd, Alma Byrd, Roy Byrd, Estelle Fox, Ernest Fox, Hazel Fox, Ira Fox, Everett Fox, Paul Fox, Esther Fox, Donald Townsend, Roy Townsend, Earl Townsend, Hoyl Townsend, Earl Climer, Dorothy Climer, Ruth Climer, two Locy children.

(They were from up north. Mr. Locy worked as a mechanic at the garage at Valle Crucis and came to help with the church. Mrs. Locy later taught school in the Banner Elk Church for one-year.)

Teacher, Olive Medford 1920–1921 and 1921–1922

Clay Clark, Viola Clark, Claude Clark, Cecil Clark, Ruby Clark, Roy Byrd, Alma Byrd, Will Byrd, Claude Byrd, Everett Fox, Loy Fox (part-time), Ira Fox, Hazel Fox, Paul Fox, Esther Fox, Ermin Fox, Dovy Fox, Donald Townsend, Roy Townsend, Earl Townsend, Hoyl Townsend, Bertha Jestes, Herman Jestes, Harry Jestes, Will Jestes, Margie Franklin, Doris Calloway, Georgia Calloway, Lola Hodges, Nanie Byrd.

Teacher, Mrs. Roberta Ingraham 1922–1923 and 1923–1924

Clay Clark, Claude Clark, Cecil Clark, Ruby Clark, Clayton Clark, Ruth Clark, Viola Clark, Lessie Watson, Helen Allen, Ira Fox, Everett Fox, Stuart Fox, Paul Fox, Esther Fox, Silas Fox, Ermin Fox, Will Byrd, Claude Byrd, Rosa Lee Byrd, Doris Calloway, Georgia Calloway, Margie Franklin, Bailey Ingraham, Edward Ingraham, Preston Ingraham, Herman Jestes, Harry Jestes, Will Jestes, Lentz Jestes, Andrew Jestes, Horace Jestes, Forrest McGinnis.

Teacher, Mrs. Mary Burdick 1924–1925 and 1925–1926

Claude Clark, Cecil Clark, Ruby Clark, Clayton Clark, Ruth Clark, Viola Clark, Hazel Teague and Allie Jenkins (both lived with the Burdicks), Will Byrd, Claude Byrd, Rosa Lee Byrd, Dick Byrd, Gordon Burdick, Esther Burdick, Hoyle Townsend, Everett Fox, Stuart Fox, Vivian Fox, Paul Fox, Esther Fox, Silas Fox, Will Jestes, Lentz Jestes, Andrew Jestes, Horace Jestes, Victoria Jestes, Marjorie Franklin, Marshall Franklin, Georgia Calloway.

Teacher, Olive Medford Clark 1926–1927

Claude Clark, Cecil Clark, Ruby Clark, Clayton Clark, Ruth Clark, Viola Clark, Will Byrd, Claude Byrd, Rosa Lee Byrd, Dock Byrd, Daisy Byrd, Margie Byrd, Stewart Fox, Vivian Fox, Margie Franklin, Marshall Franklin, it Edith Franklin, Will Jestes, Lentz Jestes, Andrew Jestes, Horace Jestes, Victoria Jestes, Lillie Jestes.

Teacher, Charles Anderson 1927–1928

Claude Clark, Cecil Clark, Ruby Clark, Clayton Clark, Ruth Clark, Will Byrd, Claude Byrd, Rosa Lee Byrd, Dock Byrd, Daisy Byrd, Stewart Fox, Vivian Fox, Lynn Fox, Margie Franklin, Marshall Franklin, it Edith Franklin, Will Jestes, Lentz Jestes, Andrew Jestes, Horace Jestes, Victoria Jestes, Lillie Jestes.

Teacher, Hazel Fox 1928–1929

Stewart Fox, Vivian Fox, Lynn Fox, Elmer Fox, Silas Fox, Ephraim Fox, Rosa Lee Byrd, Dock Byrd, Daisy Byrd, Lillie Byrd, Clyde Byrd, Claude Byrd.

Teacher, Fred Palmer 1929–930 and 1930–1931

Vivian Fox, Lynn Fox, Elmer Fox, Rosa Lee Byrd, Dock Byrd, Daisy Byrd, Lillie Byrd, Clyde Byrd, Flo Byrd, Horace Jestes, Victoria Jestes, Lillie Jestes, Ruth Clark, Winston Clark, Carl Clark.

Teacher, Dorothy Pierce 1931–1932

Ruth Clark, Winston Clark, Carl Clark, Vivian Fox, Lynn Fox, Elmer Fox, Silas Fox, Ephraim Fox, Rosa Lee Byrd, Dock Byrd, Daisy Byrd, Lillie Byrd, Clyde Byrd, Flo Byrd, Horace Jestes, Victoria Jestes, Lillie Jestes, Fannie Norwood.

Teacher, Mrs. Wellman 1932–1933

Ruth Clark, Winston Clark, Silas Fox, Ephraim Fox, Lynn Fox, Elmer Fox, Rosa Lee Byrd, Dock Byrd, Daisy Byrd, Lillie Byrd, Clyde Byrd, Flo Byrd, Horace Jestes, Victoria Jestes, Lillie Jestes, Irene Halley, Carl Clark, Wayne Clark.

Teacher, Clarence Wellman 1933–1934 and 1934–1935 (possibly other years)

Winston Clark, Carl Clark, Wayne Clark, Evelyn Clark, Rosa Lee Byrd, Dock Byrd, Lillie Byrd, Flo

Byrd, Howard Byrd, Victoria Jestes, Lillie Jestes, Lynn Fox, Elmer Fox.

Note: From 1932–1939 either Mrs. Wellman or one of her two sons, Clarence or Wallace, taught the school.

Teacher, Mr. Niverson 1940–1941

Ephraim Fox, Elmer Fox, Howard Byrd, Wayne Clark, Evelyn Clark, Ray Clark.

Teacher, Johnson 1941–1942 and 1942–1943

Betty Young, Jammie Young, Pauline Young, Eunice Young, Evelyn Clark, Ray Clark, Isabel Clark.

Teacher, Marie Holloway 1943–1944 and 1944–1945

Jammie Young, Pauline Young, Eunice Young, Isabelle Clark, Ray Clark, Norma Joan Davis, Maxine Davis.

Teacher, Mrs. H.H. Strickland 1945–1946

Jammie Young, Pauline Young, Eunice Young, Isabelle Clark, Norma Joan Davis, Maxine Davis.

Appendix V

Paths and trails

Let me tell you about the public paths in the mountains. These paths were shortcuts across mountain ridges and heads of valleys that got people where they wanted to go faster and saved miles of traveling down one valley and up another. I will guarantee these walking paths were no place for high heels and open toed shoes.

They were considered public throughways where stiles, bars or gates provided a way to get across the fences. But woe to the person who put the bars down and did not put them up again or did not leave the gate closed behind them.

Today the woods have taken back most of these old walking paths. Not even a trace of them can be found. Many times I have wished I were younger and could help mark where these old paths that crossed the mountain ridges so they would not be completely forgotten.

I have drawn a rough map to show the paths and routes those early church pioneers traveled to get to the first church on Dutch Creek.

William (Billy) Jestes and others living in Grandfather Community down Foscoe Road (now Highway 105) took a path that led over the ridge at the foot of Nettle Knob to the head of Clark's Creek. From Clark's Creek Road they took the steep path leading through Harrison Clark's cow pasture and on down to Dutch Creek Road.

Monroe Baird rode his horse or brought the buggy when Sarah came with him from Matney down the old upper Crabtree Orchard Road to the Valle Crucis Mission School (now a conference center), then took Dutch Creek road up to the church. Later he rode down the Valley Turnpike (now Highway 194).

The **Norwoods, Townsends and later the Hodges** came over the Hanging Rock Gap Road, either walking or with their wagons and teams.

Larkin Townsend and family lived on the farm now known as the Eggers place on Dutch Creek.

Columbus Fox also lived on Dutch Creek a short distance from the Dutch Creek Falls.

The **Harrison Clark** family and the **Hard Byrd** family lived on upper Clark's Creek and took the steep path through Harrison's cow pasture to get to Dutch Creek.

Alfred Townsend's family lived in the last house on Townsend Ridge Road. They saved miles of walking by taking the steep path on the Clark's Creek side of the ridge that came by the Bert Fox place, and then toiled up to the top of the steep ridge and up Clark's Creek Road (now Justice Road), over the steep ridge to Dutch Creek.

Walking path map

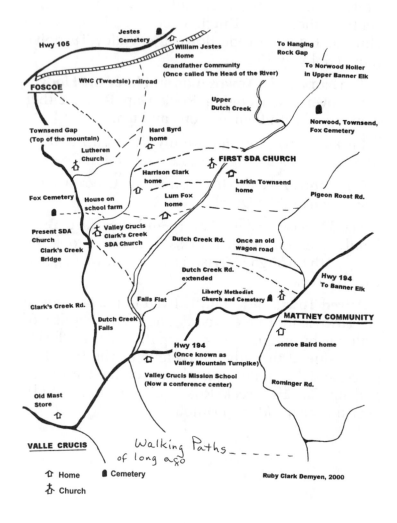

Jestes Cemetery

Hwy 105

William Jestes Home

To Hanging Rock Gap

Grandfather Community
(Once called The Head of the River)

To Norwood Holler
in Upper Banner Elk

WNC (Tweetsie) railroad

FOSCOE

Upper Dutch Creek

Norwood, Townsend, Fox Cemetery

Townsend Gap
(Top of the mountain)

Hard Byrd home

Lutheren Church

FIRST SDA CHURCH

Harrison Clark home

Larkin Townsend home

Fox Cemetery

House on school farm

Lum Fox home

Pigeon Roost Rd.

Present SDA Church

Valley Crucis Clark's Creek SDA Church

Clark's Creek Bridge

Dutch Creek Rd.

Once an old wagon road

Dutch Creek Rd. extended

Hwy 194
To Banner Elk

Clark's Creek Rd.

Falls Flat

Liberty Methodist Church and Cemetery

MATTNEY COMMUNITY

Dutch Creek Falls

Hwy 194
(Once known as Valley Mountain Turnpike)

monroe Baird home

Valley Crucis Mission School
(Now a conference center)

Rominger Rd.

Old Mast Store

VALLE CRUCIS

Walking Paths of long ago

⇧ Home   ▪ Cemetery
♁ Church

Ruby Clark Demyen, 2000

96

Appendix VI

Alphabetical list of names and places given in the text

(See also: Appendix II, Descendants of Pioneer Families; Appendix III Gravesite Locations; and a roll call of Church School students with the teachers in Appendix IV.)

A

Allen, Helen 66
Anderson, Charles and
  Ruby 57, 74
Andrews, J. N....................18
Armstrong, W. H. (Elder)
  and Gertrude.......37, 48,83
Arnette, Millard 33
Adkins, Walter Leroy.......39
Arkabour, Mr. 57
Atwell, Ruth 75

B

Baird, Alphonso...............21
Baird, Munroe 3, 6, 7, 18,
  24-28, 74
Baird, Sarah Clark 18,20,
  24
Baird, Sarah McNab 20, 21,
  55
Baird, William Carter.....20,
  21, 107
Banner Elk Church roll of
  1912................................83
Boone.............14, 66, 79, 82
Burdick, Jessie...........69, 74
Burdick, Mary......57, 69, 73
Byer, Ona 24

Byrd, Arthur......26,37,46,48
Byrd, Carson and Martha..7
Byrd, Donald 48,66
Byrd, Hard and Rosetta
  Fox..........26, 37, 46, 48, 63
Byrd, Johnny...............48,65
Byrd, Rennie 48,54
Byrd, Roy 63
Byrd, Will.....................8, 57

C

Carolina Conference........10
Calloway, John and Lottie
 83
Calloway, Robert 83
Clark, Charlie.............56, 69
Clark, Clay 52, 57
Clark, Etta........................54
Clark, Hard 63, 69
Clark, Harrison and Ellen
  White ..3, 4, 6, 7, 14,16, 23,
  29-32
Clark, Maude Baird ..15, 23,
  37, 57
Clark, Olive Medford
 57,60–66
Clark, Roby 14, 69
Clark, Wheeler 54, 63
Clark, Zettie Townsend....63

Appendix VII

Additional stories of growing up in the mountains

12/12/00

The year Santa Claus couldn't find our house
by Ruby Demyen

The year I was six and started to school for the first time — that was 1919 — our family moved. Papa sold our new home in Hoot Owl Holler in the mountains near Boone, N.C. and bought another farm on the mountain road above Clark's Creek, named for my Grandfather Clark. Mama and Papa had decided to move so my two brothers and I would not have to walk so far to attend our church school. We would also be living nearer Grandma and Grandpa. I remember the house on the new farm was an old log cabin that had been added onto.

That year, just before Christmas, Mama had been sick and in the hospital. Even though Papa worked hard every day, he barely had enough money to pay the doctor. So Mama and Papa decided they would have to skip Christmas and a visit from Santa Claus that year. On Christmas Eve no one mentioned that tomorrow was Christmas Day or even suggested we hang our stockings by the fireplace. In fact, we children were so glad Mama was well and home again that Christmas was passing by unnoticed — well almost — until...

After dinner (not a big Christmas dinner just our usual) we went to visit Grandma and Grandpa for a little while. Their house was a meeting place for all the family and several of our dozens of cousins were there, trying to out-brag each other telling about the things Santa had left in their stockings. Even our big family of Fox cousins had found small presents along with a few jokes in their stockings. Cousin Everet, who was not known to be the best little boy in school, laughed and said he found an ear of corn in his stocking. Then they asked us what we had found in ours.

On the way home from our grandparents' house my younger brother, Clayton, and I asked, "Why didn't Santa Claus come to our house, too?"

Our older brother, eight-year-old Cecil was the only one to see the painful glance Mama gave Papa and the, "You tell them," look Papa had on his face. After a moment of silence when neither one knew what to say, Mama explained, "Well, maybe since we moved Santa Claus couldn't find our new home." And that seemed to satisfy us.

Early in the next morning, before daybreak, Papa had already left for work and Mama excitedly called to us to get up and see what Santa had left on the fireboard.

"Sure enough," she said, "Santa was just late in finding us. And since your stockings are not hanging by the fireplace he has left something on the fire board for you."

We found a little mesh bag of bright colored marbles for each of us. Mama knew from eight-year-old Cecil's little half grin, as he reached for his bag of marbles, she wasn't fooling him. He had secretly told me that Santa Claus was just pretend, but I refused to believe him and of course four-year-old Clayton was still a true believer.

To add to the excitement Mama said, "If you're quiet and listen you can hear his wagon going down the road just out of sight."

We never knew where the little bags of marbles came from but they were more precious to us than a whole sleigh full of other toys.

01/07/01

Marriage in the mountains
by Ruby Demyen

Weddings were not high falutin' affairs back in my a growing up days in the Blue Ridge Mountains of N.C. That didn't mean the people were any less respectful of the marriage institution then Adam and Eve. And all the bunk you may have heard about shotgun weddings in the Li'l Abner comics of the funny papers was a big bunch of fiction.

True, girls married young in those days. My mother lacked two months of being 16 when she and my father married in 1908. But those young ladies knew the meaning of hard work and responsibility. They knew how to milk a cow, make butter, set a hen and raise chickens, and most of the other chores that went along with mountain living. They could do the washing on an old washboard in a tub and even split stove wood in an emergency. Most had already half-raised their younger brothers and sisters.

Except for a few "better off" families, where the girls sometimes managed to be able to teach at the County school, mountain girls had little chance for more schooling. Starting a married life was about their only choice.

Aside from all-day church meetings followed by dinner on the church grounds, most romances sparked during those protracted fire and brimstone meetings held in the little churches that dotted the mountain "hollers" and ridges. Those revivals were held during the fall of the year after most of the farm work was "done up."

After the meeting, a fellow would approach his favorite girl and ask if he could see her home. If this seemed to pass the test of the girl's papa, the courtship took off.

My mother and father's romance started after a Christmas program at the Valle Crucis Mission School near Boone, N.C. My father's friend, whose courtship with my mother had gone on the rocks, had asked my father to intercede for him and ask my mother if he could see her home once again. When she said, "no," my father, like John Alden, asked for himself and my mother said, "yes."

Most courting took place either on the porch swing or in the company room of the girl's home — or in the case of my mother and father, by the kitchen fireplace where they snitched her stepfather's stove wood to keep the fire in the fireplace burning brightly.

Most courtships, meaning business, did not last very long. My father faithfully courted Mama every Sunday for three months before they married. I remember how Mama's eyes sparkled when she told us about the blizzardly cold, windy Sunday morning when her sisters bet her Papa would not come to see her that day. Mama won her bet when Papa showed up about 11 a.m. riding a mule.

When the romantic young couples decided to marry they either eloped, went to the local magistrate or were married in the girl's parent's home by the church pastor. Not long ago a friend told me her parents had been married on horseback. They rode to Mast's General Store in Valle Crucis, the magistrate came out and performed the ceremony, and back home they rode.

There were no bridal showers like those given today. Instead, the couple was usually given a quilting party. My father told me how friends and neighbors all "gathered in" — the women working together to sew a quilt for the bride-to-be while the men cleared a new patch of ground for planting.

The bride usually wore a newly made dress of gingham or percale — ankle-length with a high, ruffled yoke. She wore either high-top button shoes with pointed toes or just plain, practical, shiny, black brogans.

While visiting a friend not too long ago in the old log cabin her grandfather had built and she had restored, she showed me the secret hiding place under the kitchen floor her ancestors had used to hide important documents those years ago. Several floorboards were pegged down but the pegs and boards could be removed to reveal the hiding place. Next she told me a family story about how a young bride almost went shoeless to her wedding when her sneaky little brother hid her shoes under those floor boards. Finally just before the wedding he owned up to his trick.

As for the groom's outfit, if he could afford it, he bought a new surge suit — which usually lasted him many years until he became too old and portly to wear it.

After the wedding ceremony the newlyweds usually spent their first night at the bride's home and made the trip to the groom's home the following day.

My parents told me my father borrowed a team of frisky mules and a buggy to carry my mother to his home in high style. His seven brothers and sisters and their families all waited to welcome them.

Mama recalled that grandma had the best, big dinner prepared for the whole group. (She had probably killed a couple of hens to make a big pot of chicken and dumplings to go along with all the other good dishes she put on the table, homemade from food stored in the dugout cellar or smoke house or dried and hung from the rafters.)

The young new husband and wife usually lived with the young man's parents until they could afford a place of their own. It might be a small house further up the holler from his parents or if the couple could afford it, a little house on land of their own.

I say, if they could afford it, because I once attended the 50th anniversary of a couple I knew who married with only $50 in their pocket. The marriage license cost $1.50 and the judge who married them gave it back to the bride as a gift. By hook or by crook that couple made a good life together and raised a family of six successful children.

My father and mother stayed with his parents for only about two weeks before they moved to the small, rocky farm my father had purchased in Hoot

Owl Holler near Valle Crucis. He had built a two-room house there with a promise of a larger one in the future.

I have purposely not mentioned wedding gifts earlier because in those days the gifts usually came at the time the couple moved into their own home and they were in the form of what was needed to start housekeeping on their own farm. The gifts might be a hen and rooster, ducks, Guinea fowl or a couple of geese. My father's mother gave each of her seven children the makings for their first bed — a feather tick and pillow made of feathers plucked from her own geese, quilts and a hand woven bedspread. My mother's mother gave Mama a cow.

As new couples started their married life together their love did not blind them from all the hard work and responsibility they knew lay ahead. But they were as hopeful and happily married as they would have been had the bride walked down a long church aisle wearing a $1000 wedding gown.

6/10/01

Grandfather helps a former slave with her last wish
By Ruby Clark Demyen

Most people in the western North Carolina mountains were anti-slavery and most of them remained with the Union during the Civil War. After the slaves were freed, small pockets of Black families lived in many communities.

Jane and Hosa Culver, who had been freed, lived in the Matney community. Information I received from a woman who grew up very near Matney in Pigeon Roost, Culvers were one of two Black families who lived there, one at the Eck Baird House and the other on the old Mills property.

Jane Culver stayed with white families, helping out in times of special need. She endeared herself to these families. I remember hearing my father, Roby Clark, speak fondly of the time she stayed with his family.

Mildred Gwynn, great-granddaughter of Carter William Baird who was the father of SDA Church pioneer Monroe Baird, told me the following little story when I was back in the mountains in May of 2001.

When Jane was asked if she had ever stolen anything she replied, "Not since I was freed. Before that I had to steal just to live."

Before she died she asked to be buried in the Liberty Methodist Church cemetery in Matney. But when she died, the church members were in an uproar. Some members thought, as she was a person of color, she should not be buried along with white folks in the churchyard cemetery.

Since Carter William Baird had donated the land for the church and cemetery he took the matter in hand and told them to bury her just over the fence, outside of the cemetery. Later, he moved the fence over to include Jane's gravesite. One account said he moved it one moonlit night and if that's so, perhaps it was so as not to cause more dissention among the church members, because otherwise, in my recollection of him, he was very forthright about his intentions.

Only a plain stone marked her grave but she was never forgotten. At yearly cemetery clean-off day her grave was properly cared for. On Sunday walks through the cemetery her grave was always pointed out to Baird's great grandchildren.

7/15/01

Popping buttons
by Ruby Clark Demyen

This true story happened in the early 1920's when my brothers and I were growing up in the mountains but I had no part in it. In fact, I never heard the story until May of 1991 — when actually, I heard two versions. That's really what makes it interesting.

It calls to mind the way my father could "size up" things in his own fair and honest way. And he always expected his children to tell the truth.

Before the days of good roads and cars, most people living in the mountains of western North Carolina walked and used public paths to save miles of legwork when going places. Children walking to school often used these shortcuts.

The friend who told me the first version of the story had inherited the once-thriving little mountain farm hidden on the far end of Townsend Ridge where a long line of her ancestors had lived. Even though briars and woods had almost reclaimed the farm, my friend restored the old log cabin and lived there among her fond memories of the old home.

As a child, she and her many cousins shortened their long walk to school by taking the path across the ridge and down the mountain to Clark's Creek. The public school and the nearby Seventh-day Adventist Church School let out for the day about the same time every afternoon. The children from both schools often walked home together.

One day my younger brother, Clayton, — he was about 10 — walked up the road with the public school children who lived at Townsend Ridge. When they reached the old log road turn off that led to the path across the ridge, Clayton and another boy about his age, started playfully throwing wood chips at each other as they thought up funny names to call one another.

Accidentally, (my friend said) Clayton hit the other boy with a rock, knocking him down and causing a bloody nose. She said she remembered how scared Clayton looked when he saw blood running down the boys face, but the young man was able to walk on across the ridge home with the other children.

Just before they reached their grandmother's house, someone said, "Law, Granny will be scared to death if she sees that blood." So they decided to stop at the spring and wash the blood from his face.

The next time I saw Clayton, I mentioned the story I had heard, explaining my friend said he had accidentally hit the boy in the head with a rock. Clayton's temper "flew up" at once. He said she did not tell the story straight!

He said he meant to hit the boy with that rock — it was not an accident and retorted, "I'll tell you exactly what happened."

Clayton said the boy had called him an "Old Advent" so he had meant to let him have it in the head with that rock.

Clayton went on, saying that a few days later the boy's father and an uncle or two came as a clan to our place to talk to Papa about the incident. Papa called Clayton to him and, in front of the man, asked him to tell exactly what had happened.

Clayton told Papa that the boy had called him an Old Advent and that's why he had let him have it in the head with the rock.

Papa looked down at the ground and hesitated a minute or two before saying anything. I'm sure he realized this was not just a case of a 10-year-old boy deliberately hitting another with a rock. By calling Clayton an Old Advent, the boy was expressing his clannish family's prejudice against Adventists, and a rock is usually a 10-year-old boy's handiest defense weapon. Clayton had used a rock to defend the beliefs of his family and church. (And may I add here that an unexpressed mountain code is that religion and politics are a person's own business.)

Then Papa said to Clayton, "I want you to understand once and for all time that there is to be no more rock throwing."

Clayton answered, "Yes, sir."

Turning to the men Papa said, "Now, I don't mind your children walking through my place going to school, but I want one thing clearly understood. They are to walk through and go on, minding their own business."

Evidently the men had not heard both sides of the story. As they left, Clayton knew Papa had understood and had handled the situation fairly. Even though he had been reprimanded in no uncertain terms for throwing the rock, he felt Papa had also defended him.

After almost 70 years Clayton still almost popped his buttons with boyish pride as he told his version of the story.

5/10/1998

The Pretenders
by Ruby Clark Demyen

We were 8-year-old cousins who wanted to be together every possible minute — in school, out of school, day and night. We were not only cousins, Nannie and I. We were in the same grade, going to the same school up in the rural North Carolina mountains in the early 1920s.

Miss Olive Medford taught about 25 of us, most of us first, second or third cousins, ranging in age from 6 to 14. Our one-room school was Valle Crucis Church School.

To go to school I left home about the same time Miss Medford rang the first bell at 7:30 in the morning. Usually, I could run down the mountain paths to arrive before she rang the second bell that signaled the start of the school day at 8 a.m. Unless it was during the winter when the wind might have created waist-high snow drifts. Then I needed a little extra time. Going the other way, from school to home, took a little longer because in that direction I had to climb the hills I had run down so merrily in the morning.

Everyday Nannie and I walked home from school together until we had to part, giggling along happily like only two little girls can do. I took the steep path up through the field, a shortcut to the road over the mountain from Valle Crucis to our home, just under a mile away, in Foscoe. These days, when I travel the paved, winding mountain roads by car, my heart is still skipping along mountain paths that few people, today, even imagine were once there.

When we parted, Nannie continued on the road up Clark's Creek until she came to Grandma and Grandpa's house where she stayed so she could attend our Church School. Our parting words were nearly always, "I wish you could go home with me and stay all night," even though we both knew neither Grandma nor my mama would allow us to do that all the time. The next day in school, out of loyalty to each other, we would say, "Oh, I forgot to ask for permission."

One day, as we lingered at our parting spot, our eight-year-old brains hatched up a scheme. Nannie stooped down and picked a dark-green, heart-shaped leaf from a bed of May Lilies growing beside the road. She made a little leaf cup in the palm of my hand.

Then I picked a leaf and made a matching cup in the palm of Nannie's hand. Next, we went to the little, cold, clear spring oozing out from under the roots of the hemlock trees across the road, and filled each leaf cup with that mountain water. We promised each other to carry the cups in the palms of our hands all the way home, stopping at creeks or springs along the way to put more water into the cups.

The minute Nannie got home she was to ask Grandma if she could go home with me the next night and stay all night, and the minute I got home I was to ask Mama if I could go home with Nannie. We imagined there was magic in the leaf cups that would make our wish come true.

Climbing up the steep, rough mountain paths I took going home, I tried so hard not to jiggle my hand and spill the water out of my cup. I faithfully put more water in the cup at each brook I crossed. One section of the path was so steep it seemed to go almost straight up. When I came to the fence at the top I had to crawl through the narrow space between two rough-hewn fence rails, holding on with one hand while trying to keep from spilling water out of the leaf cup in my out-stretched palm. I finely wriggled through with a few drops of water left in the cup, triumphant that the magic water remained.

Nannie's cup must have kept more of its magic though, since Grandma said "Yes," and let her come home with me after school the next day. I don't know what we would have done if both of us had been given permission to go home with the other.

Seventy-two years later at a Clark family reunion, Nannie and I enjoyed reliving our girlhood friendship and the mountain magic in our special May Lily leaf-cup pact.

2/6/1997

The Snake
by Ruby Clark Demyen

Growing up in the North Carolina mountains, my brothers and I loved being outdoors — there was always something to hold our interest and often a lesson to learn.

One day, I think it was in 1918 or so, my brothers Cecil, 7, and Clayton, 3, and I, 5, were playing in the creek right near our mountain home. With our pants legs rolled up to our knees, one of our favorite pastimes was stooping over the water watching for crawfish, then plunging our hands into the cold mountain stream trying to catch them.

On that day, all of a sudden, birds up in the big Buckeye tree shading the stream began making all kinds of noise. They seemed to be coming to the tree from every direction. They weren't singing but were flying around the tree making threatening stabs at something on the branch that hung out over the spring. They were distressed and angry and were letting everyone know it with their courageous cries.

We three children climbed out of the creek to see what was happening. That's when Cecil saw it— a snake, slithering along the tree limb toward mama robin's nest full of her babies. Mama and Papa robin were beside themselves with fear and had sent out a distress signal to the other birds for help.

The cat birds with their bright orange spots underneath their black, spreading, bobbing tails scolded that snake like mad cats, ready for a fight. The sassy mocking birds made swooping, daring darts at the snake with their flirty little tails sticking up straight in the air.

The little brown speckled wren looked the snake straight in its eyes and made feisty little jabs with its pointed sharp bill. The cardinals flushed their red feathers and threatened the snake by shaking their top knots.

The usually cheerful red-winged black birds took their turn diving and wheeling at the snake. Sparrows swarmed in from every direction, it seemed. The old blue jay, his bold beady eyes threatening Mr. Snake, squawked so loud with his rusty, raspy voice it could probably be heard all down the valley.

The snake paid very little attention to the birds, as if he knew it was all threat. He kept crawling toward the nest as Cecil ran as fast as his seven-year-old legs could carry him to get Mama. Clayton and I stood spellbound, watching, almost as scared as the birds.

Mama grabbed a hoe she kept leaning against the house near the kitchen door and came running to the tree to help the birds. But the branch that held the nest and the snake that was getting ever closer to the nest was too high for her to reach.

Soon the snake, with a big bulge in his stomach, crawled back along the branch and started his slow, coiling dissent down the tree trunk. He didn't seem to be concerned that Mama was waiting with her hoe at the bottom of the tree.

Mama often said Hoot Owl Holler, where we lived, had more snakes than anywhere she knew of and she was used to dealing with them.

When the snake reached the ground, down went her hoe on its head and it never crawled an inch further. She quickly cut the snake in half just below the swollen stomach. Oh how we wanted the little birds to still be alive. But we watched as their fuzzy, and naked little bodies with closed bulging eyes and wide open beaks tumbled out and did not move.

We wanted to cry along with the robins. Mama knew how much we cared about the baby birds and to comfort us she reminded us that God cared too. "Remember," she said, "He sees every little sparrow that falls."

5/9/1997

Praying for thunder
by Ruby Clark Demyen

Nothing could be more fun than building ponds and catching crawfish in the little mountain creek below our house. The stream chattered over rocks, dodged tree roots, splashed and dashed against big boulders, then jumped little falls on its way down Hoot Owl Holler to join the Blue Bridge Mountains' beautiful winding Watauga River just before it passed through the village of Valle Crucis.

My two brothers would roll their bib pants legs up above their knees and I, with my dress tail slapping wet, spent most of our warm summer days playing in our creek. Clayton, 3 years old, was still somewhat of a mama's boy whom Cecil, 7, and I, 5, had to watch after.

I was a tom-boy a sister born between the two boys and not yet bothered about thinking of going to school. Cecil had going to school that fall hanging over his head. He was also old enough to believe every superstitious word and every tale our teasing, laughing and loving bachelor uncle, Wheeler Clark, told him.

Want me to tell you how to catch a crawfish?

We carefully waded into the deepest part of the pond. We stood very still, trying not to stir up the mud, then stooped over and very, very carefully turned over a rock on the bottom of the pond over. We waited for the muddy water to clear so we could see any crawfish that had been hiding under the rock.

The large crawfish with their thin shell covering their backs, sharp bulging eyes near the end of their pointed nose, two long feelers sticking out from their heads, and long armed grabbing claws, were easier to catch than the little ones, which could swim backward or forward and be in a new hiding place with one flip of their little fan-shaped tails.

The large ones looked scary with their big sprawling, clumsy pinchers but they were slower moving and easier to catch. We would grab them between our thumb and fingers just behind the big claws — try as hard as they could, they could not reach our hand while we carried them and dropped them into a tin can half full of water on the bank of the creek.

Catching the little ones after the muddy water cleared was another story. Some were only an inch or two long. They were small and the color of mud so they were hard to see. Carefully and slowly we would ease our two hands to the bottom of the creek and grab them in cupped hands being careful not to lose them while the water drained away. If we did, they disappeared to a new hiding place as quick as we could bat an eye.

One day as Cecil carried a fairly large crawfish to the tin can, it flipped out of his fingers and slid down inside the front of his pants. The poor little crawfish was so scared it grabbed onto my brothers thigh with its pinchers and held on for dear life. You should have a heard Cecil wail, not only because it pinched but also because he remembered that Uncle Wheeler had warned us not to let a crawfish pinch us. He said it wouldn't let go until it thundered and there was not a cloud to be seen in the sky. We imagined the little crawfish rolling its eyes up, listening for thunder.

By the time Mama reached the creek in response to Cecil's blood curdling yell, the crawfish had decided to let go, slid to the ground and hobbled back to the creek.

When good old teasing Uncle Wheeler heard about the crawfish he hee-hawed until tears came to his eyes and was joined by our other uncles who had been helping Papa put up the hay. They teased Cecil about where the crawfish had pinched him and his thinking it wouldn't let go until it thundered.

By this time Cecil had decided maybe he shouldn't believe everything fun-loving, teasing Uncle Wheeler told him.

Copyright 2002
All Rights Reserved

We'd love to send you a free catalog of titles we publish or even hear your thoughts, reactions, criticism, about things you did or didn't like about this or any other book we publish.

Just write or call us at:

TEACH Services, Inc.
Brushton, New York 12916

1-800/367-1998

www.tsibooks.com